ABOUT THE AUTHOR

Ronald R. Liteanu, MD is a New York City adult psychiatrist with decades of experience and an Ivy League post-graduate educational background. Within his private practice, he successfully cares for patients' wellbeing, their emotional, behavioral and physical symptoms. He is inspiring people to excel and reach their greatest potential.

drronvisit.com

DISCLAIMER: This book and all its contents are for adult entertainment purposed only within the continental United States. The information provided herein is not intended, nor should it be utilized, for the diagnosis or treatment of any medical, mental, or psychological condition. Always seek the advice of your physician or other qualified healthcare provider with any questions you may have regarding a medical condition. Never disregard professional medical advice or delay in seeking it because of something you have read here. The reader agrees to indemnify and hold harmless the writer from any claim action for reader's unintended or unauthorized use of this publication.

INTRODUCTION

The enigma of clinical depression hangs over the lives of those afflicted like a heavy cloud. It is a complex and enigmatic condition that defies precise definition, its origins shrouded in a complex web of causes. Each strand in this tangled web has the power to drastically alter a person's existence, leading them down a path filled with uncertainty and despair. Like a haunting whisper, the causes of clinical depression are felt but not always seen, their impact immense and all-encompassing.

Researchers suggest that it is a combination of stressful life circumstances, trauma, and vulnerability that may contribute to the suffering of individuals. Yet, these factors are only the tip of the iceberg. Beneath the surface lies a labyrinth of changes in the brain structure, neurochemistry, genetics, comorbidities, environmental, family, social, and cultural influences, each playing a vital role in the emergence and manifestation of this elusive disorder. It is like a scattered puzzle with each piece representing a potential trigger, slowly coming together to reveal a daunting picture.

But what of those who dare to take on the challenge of understanding this complex puzzle? The clinicians, observers, analysts, and seekers of knowledge, who with each piece they discover, delve deeper into the depths of this disorder, driven by an unwavering determination to provide relief to those trapped in its grasp. But this task is no easy feat, as the puzzle is ever-evolving and the pieces constantly shifting. Along the way, research encounters a myriad of factors, each related to the complexity and unique causality of clinical depression, as well as the internal struggles and experiences of those who suffer from it.

Some are warriors, fighting against their own minds every day, while others are survivors, emerging from the darkness stronger and more resilient. The journey to understanding clinical depression evokes a range of emotions - sorrow, frustration, empathy, and hope. It is a rollercoaster of emotional battles, at times feeling like there is no end in sight. Yet, the solvers persevere, fueled by their unwavering compassion and determination, knowing that life has better moments in store. Will they succeed in their quest to unravel the mysteries of their depression? Or will its secrets remain locked away in the depths of the human psyche? Each affected individual's search continues, driven by the unbreakable bond of humanity and the relentless hope of finding relief from the darkness of their mind.

THE ISOLATION WARD

The ward nurse, Sarah, stepped into the bustling COVID-19 isolation unit, her eyes adjusting to the busy atmosphere. The ward was a labyrinth of beds, each occupied by a patient battling the relentless virus. Their labored breathing filled the air, an ever-present reminder of the fight for life happening within the four walls. As she made her rounds, Sarah's steps were purposeful, her gaze focused on each patient's condition. She navigated the ward, a witness to the impact of the enigmatic clinical depression, on these already challenging times. The stress and trauma of the pandemic served as a backdrop to the intricate web of causes that clinical depression woven, a reminder that the mind is a complex puzzle.

Among the patients, Sarah noticed a young man, David, his eyes darting anxiously, a testament to the uncertainty clinical depression brought to his life. She approached, ready to assist, when a calm, reassuring voice echoed through the ward, "Sarah, we need an update on Patient X." A colleague gestured towards David, their shared concern for his deteriorating condition evident. Sarah's training kicked in, and she swiftly gathered her notes, aware of the puzzle's ever-shifting pieces, as clinical depression presents a new challenge with each patient.

Sarah's observed David's anxious demeanor, his restlessness a clear indication of the toll Clinical depression had taken on him. Recognizing the complexity of the situation, she decided to take proactive steps. She politely excused herself from her rounds and approached the young patient, gently inquiring about his well-being. David's fidgety behavior and constant glances revealed the mystery of the disorder's grip on his life—a puzzle to be solved. Sarah requested a psychiatric consultation, knowing that an expert's insight could help piece together the clues. She wanted to confirm the diagnosis and devise a tailored plan for his recovery.

David's condition was deteriorating, and quick action was crucial. As she made the request, she noted David's vital signs, every detail recorded to provide a comprehensive update to the incoming psychiatrist. The bustling ward, a testament to the COVID-19 battle, added an extra layer of complexity to an already intricate situation. With each step, Sarah remained vigilant, aware of the ever-changing nature of clinical depression and the unique struggles it presented. Would the psychiatric consultation bring clarity and relief to the young patient or unveil further mysteries? The ward nurse, committed to her role, was determined to help navigate this complex journey.

As Sarah approached David, she noticed his anxious gaze. She knew that clinical depression, the enigmatic clinical depression, had taken hold of his mind, adding another layer of complexity to an already difficult time. The bustling ward, filled with the sounds of suffering, was a stark reminder of the puzzle she had dedicated her life to solving. She gently took David's pulse, her mind racing to piece together the mystery of his condition. The symptoms were clear, but the causes were obscure, a typical trait of clinical depression. Sarah's training taught her that this disorder, a tangled web of complications, required a multifaceted approach. As she performed her examinations, a voice interrupted her thoughts. "Nurse Sarah, we require your expertise in assessing Patient Y." A sense of urgency laced the words, prompting her to put her current patient on hold and attend to the new request. The ward was a chaotic symphony of constant demands, each life depending on the swift actions of the medical staff.

Sarah arrived beside David with concern. She rechecked his

vital signs as his breathing seemed to be rather slow a times. His pulse and temperature were normalizing. The bustling ward seemed to pause for a moment as she focused on this particular patient's condition. "Tell me about your experience," she asked, her voice soft and reassuring, aiming to create a safe space for him to share his story.

David, his eyes reflecting the weight of his struggles, began to speak. He described the darkness that had consumed him after the loss of his older brother. The pandemic had served as a cruel backdrop to his grief, amplifying his sense of isolation and despair. He felt like he was drowning in a sea of sadness, unable to find solid ground. Tears were emerging from his eyes as the was telling his story. As Sarah listened attentively, her mind began to piece together parts of the puzzle. David's story painted a clear picture of the intricate web of causes that clinical depression could weave. She knew that this disorder often hid its origins, but David's narrative provided crucial clues. She invited him to share more, each detail helping to construct his disabling condition further.

Sarah's gentle approach enabled his painful recollections. The sadness in his eyes was profound, a mirror to the depths of his despair. As he shared the devastating loss of his brother, the pandemic's cruel irony was revealed – a solitary anchor in an ocean of anguish. The ward, though still bustling with activity, seemed to pause briefly, respecting the raw emotion of the moment. Sarah's mind raced, connecting the dots between David's experiences and the enigmatic clinical depression. She encouraged him to continue, her eyes attentive, gathering every fragment she could to assemble this intricate puzzle. David, with trembling voice, described the suffocating darkness that enveloped him, a tangible presence in his everyday life. Sarah's expertise told her this was more than a simple case of grief. clinical depression's complex web had ensnared him, and she was determined to help unravel this mystery. But, as she reached out, a page came flying through the ward, seeking her attention yet again. As David continued to share his story, the enigma of his past unraveled. He revealed the profound loss of his parents years ago, and how the recent death of his brother, his only remaining close relative, had plunged him into an inescapable darkness. The ward fell briefly silent as David's words painted a poignant picture of his solitary struggle.

Sarah, ever observant, connected the dots between his experiences and the enigmatic nature of clinical depression. She knew this disorder's cunning; it hid in shadows, striking without warning. Yet, something about this case intrigued her, perhaps the timing of the pandemic, or the complexity of his circumstances. As David described the suffocating grip of depression, Sarah's determination grew stronger. She made a silent promise to help him, to navigate the maze of his mind and offer a path to healing. But as she turned to gather her thoughts, a sense of urgency filled the ward once more. Another patient required her attention, an urgent reminder of the bustling COVID-19 unit and its relentless demands.

The nurse's ward is a chaotic battlefield, where the war against COVID-19 rages on. Amidst this crisis, another formidable mental foe looms and creeps into the ward, adding an extra layer of complexity to an already demanding situation. Sarah, the diligent nurse, finds herself drawn to listen to the young patient, whose anxious eyes reflect the turmoil within. As she reaches out, another urgent call for assistance interrupts her, pulling her attention away momentarily. The ward demands her presence elsewhere, but her mind remains fixated on David and the mysteries unfolding within his mind. David, burdened by grief, paints a tragic picture of his life. He speaks of the darkness that enveloped him after the pandemic took his brother, leaving him alone to battle the shadows. His voice, trembling with emotion, reveals the depth of his despair, an echo of the loneliness that consumes him. The ward falls silent, the bustling activity momentarily paused, as David's words cast a spell of compassion on those who hear them. Sarah's determined gaze never wavers as she listens intently, the pieces of this intricate puzzle slowly clicking into place.

As the story of depression's mystery continues, we find ourselves delving into the tragic tale of an individual whose struggles have reached their pinnacle. Overwhelmed by grief and sorrow, his once vibrant energy and interests have faded into obscurity. The darkness of his suffering mind has consumed him, leading them to contemplate the unthinkable - suicide. This plight is not unique; many are entangled in the same crushing grip of despair. Some battle daily, a silent war within their minds, while others, like survivors of a treacherous journey, emerge strengthened from the depths of darkness.

But amidst this gloom, there are those who strive to understand and help. Clinicians, researchers, and compassionate souls dedicate themselves to this enigmatic disorder, seeking to unravel its intricate web of causes. As they gather the scattered pieces of this puzzle, they find themselves engaged in a relentless pursuit, akin to a game of cat and mouse, where the target constantly eludes them. The complexities of clinical depression are indeed a daunting challenge.

David's words painted a tragic picture, his voice cracking with emotion as he revealed the darkest depths of his despair. As the ward fell silent, a hushed respect descended upon the room, and Sarah's eyes remained locked on David, determined to unravel this perplexing case.

The mysteries of the mind were her forte, and she refused to be deterred by the chaos unfolding around her. Yet, amidst the ward's clamor, another urgent situation demanded her attention. Should she prioritize David's growing crisis or attend to the new emergency? The decisions made in this moment could shape David's journey towards healing or further mystery. As Sarah faced this crucial juncture, she glanced towards David, his eyes pleading for help, and the bustling ward seemed to pause, awaiting her next move.

As David's tragic tale continued to unfold, painting a dire picture of the depths he had sunk into, Sarah recognized the gravity of the situation. She promptly called for reinforcement, requesting an additional nurse to tend to the ward's other patients so she could focus on this urgent case. David's despair, amplified by the pandemic's cruel twist of fate, demanded immediate action.

With the backup nurse now by her side, Sarah dedicated her full attention to the young patient, determined to unravel the mysteries behind his decline. The ward, though still a hive of activity, seemed to respect the gravity of this moment, its pace slowing just a fraction as if in hushed contemplation. Sarah's sharp eyes and expert training connected the dots, recognizing the intricate dance of Clinical depression amidst David's anguish. As he spoke of the darkness that consumed him, Sarah embarked her attention to his distressing condition. She responded with a gentle approach, her actions a blend of medical expertise and compassionate understanding, guiding him towards the bright window facing his room. She provided him with her intuitive, compassionate and intense focus.

David's glaring eyes were pleading for relief from the torment that consumed him. His mind was shrouded in the enigmatic grasp of clinical depression. While the ward's chaotic atmosphere seemed to swirl around us, the emerging psychiatrist, Dr. Jones, focused his attention on David's plight.

As he shared his story, a tragic tale unfolded. David spoke of the darkness that had overtaken him, a darkness that was amplified by the cruel timing of the pandemic. The loss of his brother, his sole remaining relative, had left him alone in a world of grief. His once vibrant artistic spirit had faded, and the shadows of despair threatened to engulf him entirely. Dr. Jones listened intently, each detail painting a clearer picture of the complex web that depression had woven around him.

Dr. Jones requested David share more, and as he did, a new layer of mystery emerged. He described the solitude of his existence, how the pandemic had isolated him further, and the overwhelming sense of being alone with his sorrow. Time seemed to stand still as the ward fell silent, absorbing the raw emotion of his narrative. The psychiatrist observed his every word, connecting the dots to the enigma that was clinical depression. The doctor knew that this disorder's origins were often shrouded, but David's experiences provided a unique window into his circumstances. David's symptoms were clear, and his story, a tragic narrative of loss and despair, painted a vivid picture of the intricate web of depression.

As the ward fell silent once more, a sense of focus and determination settled upon it. Sarah and Dr. Jones stood alongside David, his tale of darkness and solitude having touched those around him. With the ward's chaos momentarily forgotten, they attended to his immediate needs, recognizing the complex symptoms of his severe depression. David's struggles, amplified by the pandemic, had led him to the brink, and their collective goal was to navigate him towards the light.

Sarah's sharp eyes scanned the ward, observing David's desperate plea for help amidst the chaos of the bustling COVID-19 unit. Recognizing the severity of his condition, she swiftly took action. As David's symptoms became more apparent—his restlessness, lack of appetite, and difficulty concentrating—Sarah knew that this was a critical situation that required her full attention.

The ward, a bustling hub of activity, seemed to stand still as Sarah's determined gaze remained fixed on David. She was there with Dr. Jones assessing the patient's serious condition. Together, they approached David, and as his tragic tale unfolded, the enigma of clinical depression became increasingly evident. Dr. Jones listened intently, every detail painting a grim picture of David's solitary struggle.

The ward fell silent as David's story touched the hearts of all who heard it. He spoke of the darkness that had consumed him, a darkness that the pandemic had amplified, leaving him feeling isolated and alone. As David's voice cracked with emotion, Sarah and Dr. Jones connected the dots, recognizing the complex web of depression that had ensnared him. They identified the classic symptoms: poor sleep, feelings of guilt and shame, a lack of energy, and emerging suicidal thoughts. Determined to offer a glimmer of hope, Sarah and the psychiatrist devised a comprehensive plan for his recovery, prioritizing David's urgent crisis.

David's respiratory issues began to subside, allowing him the respite of short walks outside the ward. Accompanied by Sarah, these excursions provided a temporary escape from the confines of the bustling unit. Sarah, with her social work degree and compassionate nature, was determined to guide him towards recovery. David's story, a narrative of loss and despair, remained a constant reminder of the intricate web of depression's causes.

Amidst the ward's relentless activity, a focused determination settled over Sarah and Dr. Jones as they devised a comprehensive strategy aimed at David's restoration. The pandemic's cruel ironies were ever-present, yet the prospect of hope emerged as a guiding light in the face of this enigmatic disorder.

Dr. Jones listened intently to David's tragic tale; his eyes fixed on the patient as he spoke of the overwhelming darkness that had consumed his life. The physician's mind began to formulate a plan, one that would counteract David's despair. He prescribed a powerful antidepressant to alleviate the crushing weight of depression and crafted a specialized diet regimen, tailored to nourish David's depleted body and mind. This plan included essential vitamins and nutrients known to aid in mental health and promote overall well-being.

Alongside Sarah, the psychiatrist encouraged David to take short, restorative walks outside the ward, a temporary sanctuary from the constant bustle inside. During these excursions, David found momentary peace, a respite from the relentless grip of his thoughts.

Back inside the ward, Sarah's compassionate nature shone through as she diligently supported David, while Dr. Jones' determined focus steered their collective efforts. They worked together to implement a comprehensive strategy aimed at David's recovery, acknowledging the intricate web of depression's causes and the unique circumstances brought on by the pandemic.

In the midst of this complex situation, a glimmer of hope emerged. With each passing day, David responded positively to the treatment, showing gradual signs of improvement. The darkness that had once consumed him seemed to lift, like the dawn of a new day breaking through the night. Though the ward remained a hub of activity, a sense of optimism settled over David's situation, offering a ray of light in the battle against the enigmatic clinical depression.

David's plight continued to unfold amidst the chaotic ward, his eyes pleading for a respite from the torment of his mind. As Sarah and Dr. Jones continuously attended to his growing needs, the enigma of clinical depression revealed itself in every detail. Sarah and the physician's faces grew more determined as David shared his story, a harrowing narrative of darkness and solitude amplified by the pandemic's cruel ironies.

The duo's unwavering dedication began to show positive results as David responded well to the treatment. The darkness that had once shrouded his world seemed to lift, allowing him to find solace in his beloved art supplies that he was now able to use in the ward. Hope blossomed amidst the gloom as they witnessed his gradual return to a path of healing.

David's desperate gaze pleaded for a release from the torment that consumed his very being. Nurse Sarah and Dr. Jones remained steadfast in their mission to bring him solace, understanding the intricacies of his predicament. As the ward buzzed with activity, they focused intently on David's journey, an epic battle against the enigmatic clinical depression.

Sarah's compassionate nature and Dr. Jones' determined approach guided David toward a glimmer of hope on the horizon. They encouraged him to find solace in his beloved art, and soon his canvases were filled with vibrant hues, reflecting his gradual return to life. The pandemic's cruel grip may have triggered his descent into darkness, but the duo's unwavering support became a beacon, steering him away from the edge.

With each passing day, David's spirit revived, his appetite for life slowly returning. The ward's chaotic atmosphere, though ever-present, seemed to recede as a peaceful resolve settled upon him. Sarah and Dr. Jones' collaboration had yielded positive results, the mysteries of clinical depression slowly unraveled, and a sense of victory emerged from the depths of despair.

David, his eyes now filled with a glimmer of hope, continued to find solace in his art. As he was provided with his cherished art supplies, a sense of peace seemed to wash over him. A fellow patient, an amiable figure who is passionate about art, approached him one day. With a gentle smile, this companion invited him on a refreshing walk to the nearby park. David, grasping his easel and paints, joined this friend for an afternoon of tranquility amidst the green expanse. As they strolled, David found himself increasingly immersed in a world of beauty and calm, a welcome escape from the ward's enigmatic chaos.

Meanwhile, Nurse Sarah and Dr. Jones, ever vigilant in their pursuit of helping David, witnessed his gradual transformation with quiet determination. They had seen the darkness that enveloped him and were committed to guiding him towards the light, pursuing a life-changing mission.

Nurse Sarah and Dr. Jones, ever vigilant in their determined mission, observed David's gradual revival with a quiet yet determined resolve. Using their combined expertise towards a common goal.

As the two artists returned from their rejuvenating excursion, they found themselves drawn into a rich conversation about their shared love for art. They spoke of the ward's enigmatic nature and the transformative power of their creative outlet. David's eyes sparkled with a new-found determination as he contemplated the possibility of a joint artistic endeavor—a collaboration born out of shared experiences. And so, amidst the ward's relentless bustle, a subtle shift occurred, bringing a renewed sense of purpose to David and planting a thriving seed of hope in the hearts of those who witnessed his transformation.

David's journey toward recovery continued alongside the unwavering dedication of Nurse Sarah and Dr. Jones. As the trio formed an unbreakable bond, they navigated the intricate web of David's depression, always mindful of the ever-present COVID-19 ward and its relentless demands.

As David's condition improved, Sarah and the psychiatrist devised a plan for his gradual discharge from the ward. Yet, their shared passion for art left a lasting impression, inspiring the two men to collaborate on a creative endeavor that would change their lives forever. Together, they left the ward, embarking on a new chapter, while Sarah and Dr. Jones remained vigilant in their support, ensuring his seamless transition to outpatient care.

David, now filled with a renewed sense of purpose, found solace in his newfound friendship and their shared love for creativity. They decided to establish an art studio, a haven where their talents could thrive and inspire. Their unique experiences served as the perfect foundation for their artistic collaboration, and soon they were creating breathtaking works that captivated clients and patrons alike. Amidst the chaos of the pandemic, a glimmer of hope and beauty emerged, offering a powerful testament to the resilience of the human spirit.

With each passing day, David's spirit soared, and his recovery gained momentum. He found joy in the simple act of walking his loyal companion, a lovable dog rescued from the local shelter. The ward, though always busy, seemed to fade into the background as David's world became increasingly filled with brighter colors and life. Meanwhile, Nurse Sarah and Dr. Jones witnessed this transformation with quiet pride, knowing that their collective efforts had helped steer David away from the darkest depths.

The art studio buzzed with activity as the two artists' reputations grew. Their unique partnership became a beacon of hope, a testament to the power of art and the enduring human spirit. As they continued their respective journeys, the ward remained a chaotic yet sacred space, where the battle against depression and the pandemic raged on, and the dedicated staff, including Sarah and Dr. Jones, remained steadfast in their mission to bring solace and healing.

THE BED CONFINEMENT

Thomas' situation remained a mystery to the medical professionals as his condition persisted despite numerous attempts at treatment. Dr. Healy, aware of the complexity of the case, reached out to Dr. Paterson, an esteemed psychiatrist, for guidance. The latter immediately scheduled a consultation with Thomas, aiming to delve deeper into his patient's psyche and uncover the roots of his despair.

The doctors' efforts to aid Thomas were unwavering as they acknowledged the challenges of treating his condition. Dr. Paterson's expert eyes observed Thomas' demeanor, recognizing the depth of his anguish and the enigma surrounding its causes. The psychiatrist's approach was meticulous as he knew the intricacies of depression's web; he spent time unraveling Thomas' story, a tale laden with sorrow.

Thomas, an always robust individual, described the gradual descent into darkness that had consumed him over a three months' time. The loss of his energy, appetite, and interest in his work painted a dire picture of the toll depression had taken. His words echoed the despair he felt, a despair that had confined him to his bed for months, leaving him a mere shadow of himself. The doctors listened intently, each detail drawing them closer to understanding the puzzle's pieces.

Dr. Paterson's consultation with Thomas delved deep into his past, unearthing the layers of his psyche. The middle-aged man's once vibrant spirit had been diminished by a gradual descent into darkness, shrouding him for three months. This gloom had robbed Thomas of his energy, appetite, and enthusiasm for his work, transforming him into a shadow of his former self. Confined to his bed, the weight of depression pulled him deeper into a bottomless pit of despair.

The meticulous psychiatrist listened intently as Thomas recounted the gradual loss of himself, his words echoing the depth of his anguish. Alongside Dr. Healy, they explored the mysteries of Thomas' mind, recognizing the intricate web of depression's origins. His past unraveled, revealing a devoted family man, his world turned upside down by unforeseen circumstances. The doctors were determined to unravel this enigma, armed with the knowledge that depression's roots could be elusive, often lurking in the shadows.

As the consultation progressed, the doctors' faces grew more determined. They devised a revised treatment plan, tailored to Thomas' unique situation. This approach would incorporate a meticulous strategy to address the underlying causes. The doctors' unwavering dedication offered a glimmer of hope, a potential light at the end of the tunnel for Thomas' journey towards healing.

Dr. Paterson's eyes remained fixed on Thomas as he shared his distressing story, a tragic narrative of gradual descent into darkness. The middle-aged man spoke of his new life in America, the land of hope from his native Cuba, and the crushing disappointment that followed. Thomas' voice trembled with emotion as he recounted the high expectations he had for his new beginning, only to be brought low by the enigmatic grip of depression. alongside Dr. Healy, Paterson listened intently, their concerned faces as they absorbed the patient's words, each detail painting a clearer, yet still murky, picture.

The doctors were aware of the intricate web of depression's

origins, and Thomas' story only confirmed the complexity of his condition. As he described the loss of his energy and appetite, the two physicians exchanged a glance, their determination growing stronger. They had encountered Thomas' situation before, the mysteries of depression never ceasing to challenge them. Yet, with each case, they approached the enigma with renewed fervor, armed with the knowledge that every patient held a unique key to unlocking the causes. Thomas' circumstances were no different, and the doctors devised a strategy tailored to his experiences.

The revised treatment plan was meticulous, designed to address the underlying causes and the symptoms that had confined Thomas to his bed. The doctors' expertise and unwavering dedication offered a glimmer of hope, a potential path to recovery. As Thomas concluded his narrative, the ward fell briefly silent, the weight of his words hanging in the air. Dr. Paterson assured him that together, they would navigate this complex journey, and Thomas, though skeptical, grasped onto the prospect of healing. The puzzle of his mind was intricate, but the doctors were seasoned in unraveling such mysteries.

Thomas' meticulous preparation for his doctor's appointments, donning a suit and tie with a fresh haircut, added an intriguing layer to the puzzle. The doctors were intrigued by being led to believe that Thomas was working at AT&T as an office executive.

The revelation of Thomas' true occupation came as a surprise. He was not the office executive they had envisioned but a diligent lineman who tirelessly worked in AT&T's cable division. His daily labor involved scaling tall utility poles and navigating through wooded areas, an unknown hero connecting the threads of communication. This unexpected revelation shifted the doctors' perspective, opening their eyes to the possibility of depression's complex origins.

With each detail, the doctors connected the dots, piecing together the puzzle of Thomas' plight. The origins of his depression, though complex and multifaceted, were being slowly revealed. Dr. Paterson's and Dr. Healy's collective experience promised a meticulous approach to Thomas' condition.

Thomas' lineman work was in the wooded areas of the northeastern United States, a region known for its high concentration of ticks, carriers of Lyme disease, a slow-creeping parasite that could cloud the mind and steal one's vitality.

Thomas knew the potential risks posed by the ticks. He took his precautions, always spraying his clothing with insect repellent and covering his skin whenever he ventured out. Still, there was only so much one may do when working in such an environment.

Each day, Thomas woke up with a sense of dread, knowing the threat of losing his job as his depression worsened and he was glued to his bed. The constant threat of this disease loomed over him, a dark cloud hovering, ready to pour its frustration and lethargy upon him.

As the story of Thomas' enigmatic depression unfolded, the doctors homed in on a surprising revelation – his true occupation as a lineman for AT&T. This new information threw them off balance, as it exposed the possible culprit that had led to his decline. The physical demands of Thomas' work, combined with the risk of Lyme disease, painted a new picture of the origins of his illness.

The revelation about Thomas' job shed light on the intricate puzzle of his condition. The doctors now understood the physical and psychological toll his work had exacted, with the risk of contracting Lyme disease adding an extra layer of stress and anxiety. This knowledge propelled them to act swiftly. Blood test results confirmed the presence of the disease, providing a new direction for treatment.

Despite the growing complexities, Dr. Healy and Dr. Paterson remained resolute in their pursuit of relief for Thomas. They revised their approach, implementing a meticulous strategy aimed at tackling the depression's root causes. With this new insight, they crafted a treatment plan that acknowledged the interplay of Thomas' physical and mental health. The origins of Thomas' deep depression, shrouded in mystery, were now being illuminated, offering a renewed sense of direction in their quest for his recovery.

The medical professionals had been baffled by Thomas' persistent condition, which seemed unaffected by various treatment attempts. His situation was an enigma, a complex puzzle with pieces scattered across the intricacies of his life. As Dr. Healy and Dr. Paterson delved deeper, they discovered a tale of two contrasting lives, both laden with their own share of struggles.

Thomas, a diligent worker, had led the doctors to believe he was a suit-and-tie office executive at AT&T. This perception was carefully crafted by Thomas, who took pride in his meticulous presentation. However, the truth unfolded, revealing a different story. Thomas was a lineman, a behind-the-scenes hero who braved the great outdoors and climbed towering utility poles in the midst of heavily wooded areas.. This revelation surprised the doctors, who now understood the hidden exposed risks of his work.

The risks of Thomas' occupation became a critical piece in the depression puzzle. His job, with its tick exposure in wooded areas, pointed towards Lyme disease, a sneaky culprit that could steal energy and vitality without obvious signs. The doctors had been adept at recognizing this disease's subtle hints, and so they acted swiftly. Blood tests confirmed the presence of the disease, providing a new direction for treatment and a renewed sense of hope for Thomas' recovery. They revised their strategy, tailoring it to the newly discovered physical and psychological aspects of his condition. As the pieces of the puzzle fell into place, a comprehensive plan emerged to combat the roots of Thomas' despair.

Lyme disease, a bacterial infection, transmitted by ticks prevalent in wooded areas, had taken a persistent toll on Thomas' physical and mental well-being. The bacterium, Borrelia burgdorferi, is known for its elusive nature, often evading detection until it had inflicted severe damage.

Recognizing the disease's subtle hints, the doctors acted promptly. Blood tests confirmed the presence of Lyme disease, offering a new perspective for treatment. They knew that prompt and effective intravenous administration of the appropriate antibiotics could make all the difference. The susceptibility of B. burgdorferi to specific antibiotics had to be carefully evaluated to determine the most suitable course of action. Time was of the essence, as Thomas' condition persisted, a complex interplay of physical ailment and deepening despair.

A renewed and focused determination settled over the medical professionals as they revised Thomas' treatment plan. They were now armed with a new understanding of the causes underlying his depression, a condition that had extensively confined him to his bed.

With each passing day, the doctors' unwavering dedication and meticulous approach brought them closer to unlocking the mysteries of Thomas' mind and body. Despite the emerging complexities, and Thomas' known allergy to penicillin, the doctors remained resolute in their pursuit of Thomas' relief and recovery. Their experience allowed them to develop a revised treatment strategy, addressing the physical and psychological dimensions of his depression. With each passing day, their dedication and meticulous approach brought them closer to relive Thomas' his miserably depressing condition.

The doctors now navigated a revised landscape. Thomas' hospitalization and intensive antibiotic regime began, alongside a depression treatment plan tailored to his circumstances. The doctors' unwavering dedication bore fruit as Thomas' condition improved daily. The clouds of despair lifted, and a renewed Thomas emerged from the depths of his illness, grateful for the unwavering support.

Thomas lay in his hospital bed, surrounded by the comforting presence of his loved ones. His spouse, ever diligent, prepared nutritious meals under the watchful guidance of the medical staff, who were determined to aid Thomas's full recovery. The nurses were unwavering in their support, encouraging him to take those first renewed steps out of bed and towards health.

The children brought life and energy to the room, their playful antics serving as a delightful distraction from the mundane hospital routine. Their presence brought a sense of home into the sterile environment, lifting Thomas's spirits as he laughed and interacted with them, a welcome change from the monotonous hours of recuperation.

Each day, Thomas's strength returned, a testament to the dedicated care and love surrounding him. The gravity of his illness was not lost on those around him, and the collective hope for his recovery served as a powerful motivator. With each passing day, Thomas inched closer to health, his progress steady, guided by the unwavering support of his family, the doctors, skilled nurses, and the comforting familiarity of home-cooked meals.

As the doctors continued their meticulous work, they remained oblivious to the impact their revised strategy would have on Thomas' life. The revelation of his true occupation as a lineman had been a crucial piece in the puzzle of his depression, and with the Lyme disease diagnosis, they now had a clear direction to Thomas' recovery.

The doctors and nurses, ever vigilant in their duties, guided Thomas towards recovery, their dedication evident in his gradual return to health. Each day, Thomas' strength returned to him slowly, like a long-lost friend, as the clouds of despair lifted. He found solace in the company of his loved ones, who surrounded him with unwavering support and a sense of home.

Thomas' return to work after his illness was met with a heartfelt welcome from his teammates and supervisors, who were relieved to have him back. They gathered around him, sharing stories of the work he had missed and catching him up on the projects he would now rejoin. Thomas felt a renewed sense of purpose as he listened, determined to contribute once more to the team he had briefly left behind.

Thomas persevered, eager to reacquaint himself with his missed role. As he settled back into his routine, the familiar feeling of supporting his family through his work emerged, giving him a sense of fulfillment. The kindness shown to him by his colleagues helped ease his transition, and he found solace in the knowledge that he was not alone in his past struggles.

Each day, Thomas' confidence grew as he reconnected with his old duties and discovered new challenges. The support he received from his loved ones and colleagues enabled him to approach his work with a fresh perspective. Though the experience had been arduous, Thomas emerged with a deeper appreciation for his role and the impact he has on all those around him. The puzzle pieces of his life were slowly fitting back together, and the enigma that had bed confinement him have been fading away.

THE COVERT IMPOSTOR

An enigmatic figure, Mark, stood apart from the bustling crowd, his eyes reflecting the weight of the world. The busy executive had always found it difficult to shake off the stresses of the workday, and as the weight of his responsibilities bore down on him, he reached for the familiar solace of hard alcohol. It was a ritual that had been passed down through generations, a toxic legacy that now threatened to consume him.

As Mark's habits grew more pronounced, so did his feelings of anxiety and despair. The crowd dispersed, leaving him alone with his thoughts, a solitary figure haunted by his past and present. The ward, usually a bustling hub of activity, seemed to pause, its rhythm momentarily disrupted by Mark's presence. Nurse Sarah, ever vigilant, noticed Mark's deteriorating state and took proactive steps toward his aid.

Recognizing the complex interplay of work stress, genetic predispositions, and Mark's increasing reliance on alcohol, the nurse requested a consultation with the psychiatrist. The mental health professional arrived promptly, aware of the delicate nature of Mark's situation, and initiated a thorough assessment. Their objective eyes observed Mark's anxious demeanor and the telltale signs of declining mental health. The psychiatrist's experienced gaze delved deeper, probing Mark's family history and the cyclical nature of his struggles, while the nurse attended to his vital signs, an ever-present support.

Mark's story, a tragic narrative of stress and surrender, unfolded before them. The origins of his despair, layered and intricate, were laid bare. Together, the medical professionals crafted a comprehensive plan, a beacon of hope in the darkening storm of Mark's mind. The first steps toward recovery were often the hardest, but with the support of the nurse and psychiatrist, Mark embarked on a journey of healing, guided by the light of their expertise and compassion.

Mark's story continued to unfold before the attentive nurse and the psychiatrist. As they delved deeper into his recent struggles, a new layer of complexity emerged. Mark had been grappling with the imposter syndrome, a poisonous thought loop that questioned his every accomplishment and amplified his self-doubt. The more he tried to shake off these nagging thoughts, the more they consumed him, fueling his anxiety and depression.

These feelings manifested as a dark cloud that followed him, a constant reminder of his perceived fraudulence in the face of his rapid professional advancement.

The weight of this internal struggle intensified his reliance on alcohol, hoping to find temporary solace in its bottomless pit. Nurse Sarah and the psychiatrist couldn't help but notice the correlation between Mark's downward spiral and his recent promotion at work. They observed how the pressure to maintain his new status only intensified his feelings of inadequacy and shame.

Mark's story was one of many such tales, a tragic reminder of the delicate balance between success and surrender. However, amidst the gloom, there was a glimmer of hope. The psychiatrist and nurse devised a strategy to help Mark navigate his way through the labyrinth of imposter thoughts, equipping him with tools to challenge this toxic mindset. With their guidance, Mark embarked on a journey of self-discovery, learning to dispel the clouds of doubt that darkened his mind.

Mark's past and present intertwined, a tangled web of memories and feelings. The favoritism he'd experienced from his teacher in his childhood came back to him as a distant, yet vivid, memory. He had always wanted to impress her, afraid of disappointment. It was a feeling that had driven him to excel in his studies, but also one that had caused him to resort to little white lies when he couldn't comprehend the complex homework assignments.

That same sense of inadequacy had followed him into adulthood, manifesting in the form of imposter syndrome as his career progressed. Mark felt a fraud, especially after a recent promotion, and the weight of it all pushed him closer to the edge. The bustling executive stood alone, his eyes carrying the burden of the world. Yet, amidst the gloom, there was hope on the horizon.

Nurse Sarah's vigilant eye had caught Mark's descent, and now, with the psychiatrist's assessment, they aimed to guide him towards a different path. One of self-acceptance and truth. The mental health professional delved into Mark's memories of his childhood, the advanced tasks set by his teacher, and the feelings of embarrassment that had driven him to dissemble. It was a crucial layer of the puzzle, unlocking understanding and a tailored strategy to help Mark confront and challenge his inner deceptions.

Mark's story, a tragic tale of stress and addiction, unfolded. Mark had battled with feelings of inadequacy and anxiety for as long as he could remember, a constant companion to his success. These feelings were only amplified by his recent rapid professional rise, marking him with the imposter syndrome. A dark cloud of self-doubt followed Mark. Nurse Sarah and the attentive psychiatrist observed Mark's telling of his downward spiral with growing concern, recognizing his added intricacies to his condition.

As Mark recounted his college days, he recalled the frequent drinking sessions with his fraternity brothers, a temporary escape from the panic attacks and intense feelings of inadequacy that plagued him. The more Mark tried to shake off these feelings, the more they consumed him, creating a vicious cycle that led him to the brink of destruction.

Nurse Sarah and the psychiatrist listened intently, their eyes darting between Mark and each other, both aware of the critical role alcohol had played throughout Mark's life. They delved further, probing Mark's relationship with his family and the influences that shaped his childhood. Mark's words painted a picture of a troubled past, and the professionals began to piece together the puzzle of his experiences. The imposter syndrome, fed by Mark's insecurities, had grown into a dark cloud, shadowing his every achievement. The roots ran deep, and the psychiatrist's experienced gaze uncovered a trail of breadcrumbs leading back to Mark's earliest memories.

The professionals traced the origins of Mark's problems back to his childhood, where they discovered a significant correlation between his interactions with alcohol and his feelings of inadequacy. Mark revealed that alcohol had been a constant in his life, an easy crutch to lean on since the age of eleven. It was a coping mechanism, an attempt to quell the anxiety and panic attacks that had begun to accompany his sense of inadequacy. This revelation shed light on the deeper roots of Mark's issues, as the psychiatrist and nurse connected these early experiences with his current battle against the imposter syndrome.

It seemed that Mark's past had come back to haunt him, the problems of his youth exacerbating his present struggles. Yet, the uncovering of these long-held secrets, these hidden demons, offered a crucial key to unlocking Mark's recovery. With this new understanding, the mental health professionals tailored their approach, aiming to help Mark confront his past and finally break free from the toxic cycle that had brought him to the brink.

The executive's daily grind had been a strain on his shoulders, and the stresses of the workday often lingered. Mark was attended self-help meetings, where he found camaraderie among strangers who shared his struggles. He found peace in telling his story, and hope in the success stories of those who had recovered. The support group's atmosphere provided a comforting sanctuary, a contrast to the perceptively demanding outside world. As Mark stood, reflecting on his thought, the internal room lights reflected in his eyes, casting a gleam that hinted at a hidden determination.

Mark's story of stress and addiction continued to unfold. As the psychiatrist and Nurse Sarah delved deeper, they suggested an approach that could help Mark battle his demons. They recommended Mark attend the self-help group sessions, specifically designed for those grappling with alcohol addiction.

Mark heeded their advice and found himself sitting in on a Support Group meeting, an assortment of strangers whose stories echoed his own. The room was filled with tales of struggle and hope, a stark contrast to the solitary despair Mark had known. As he listened, a sense of camaraderie grew within him. Mark found solace in the shared experiences, a comforting realization that he was not alone in his battle. The group's atmosphere provided a safe haven from the pressures of the outside world, a sanctuary where Mark could unburden himself.

The group sessions became a regular routine, a welcome escape from the relentless pace of his workday life. Mark discovered a new sense of purpose and determination within the group's supportive environment. The stories of recovered addicted individuals inspired him, none more so than his sponsor, who had maintained sobriety for a decade. Mark began to see a glimmer of hope in the midst of his own dark clouds, a chance to break free from the shackles of his past. Each new meeting brought him closer to accepting his true self, a journey of self-discovery and healing that unfolded with each shared story.

Mark's story of struggle and redemption continued to further unfold before the attentive nurse, Sarah, and the insightful psychiatrist. Their collective efforts to help Mark delved deeper into the realms of his past, unearthing pivotal moments that shaped his trajectory. Amidst the revelations, one particular aspect stood out: the influence of a significant other. Mark, it seemed, had found solace and reinforcement in the arms of a loving fiancée. She served as his beacon of hope, a constant reminder of his inherent strength. Mark had confided in her about his secret battles with sobriety, sharing the pivotal role alcohol had played in his life since his teenage years.

The fiancée, a supportive pillar, recalled the early days of their relationship, when Mark had achieved a remarkable six months of sobriety, a testament to his willpower. That milestone had solidified their budding romance. However, the pressures of Mark's executive lifestyle and the demons he fought had led him back to alcohol in secrecy. The strain of balancing his work and personal life had become a heavy burden. Yet, with the support of his fiancée, the secrets were laid bare, and a new path toward healing began to emerge. She encouraged him, reminding Mark of his past triumphs over adversity. The psychiatrist and Nurse Sarah witnessed the positive influence this partner had on Mark's psyche, adding a new dimension to their tailored approach. Together, they encouraged Mark to harness this relationship, using it as a catalyst for change.

Mark's journey following his discharge from the hospital continued on a path of self-improvement and discovery. Under the care of an outpatient psychiatrist, his treatment for anxiety and depression advanced alongside his attendance at self-help group meetings. These meetings became a staple of his routine, a sanctuary from the challenges of his everyday life.

The influence of his supportive fiancée remained a constant source of encouragement, reminding Mark of his past successes and fostering hope for the future. Her unwavering support was another pivotal element in Mark's recovery, reinforcing the lessons he learned in therapy and the determination to maintain his sobriety. As Mark pressed on with his outpatient treatment, the psychiatrist skillfully delved into the roots of Mark's anxiety and the imposter syndrome that had consumed him.

Mark's journey into self-discovery and healing continued under the watchful eyes of the outpatient psychiatrist. Mark's therapy delved deeper into the roots of his anxiety and the imposter feelings that had plagued him for so long. The psychiatrist's expert probing helped uncover the formative experiences that shaped Mark's perceptions.

The primary objectives of the therapy remained focused on assisting Mark in his battle against the imposter syndrome, low self-esteem, and the fears of failure and success that plagued him. The psychiatrist employed a multitude of approaches to address these core issues, often exploring the roots of Mark's anxiety through thoughtful inquiries.

As Mark's therapy progressed, the psychiatrist continued to introduce new techniques to challenge Mark's negative thought patterns and the feelings of inadequacy that arose during his workday. He was empowered to stand taller in the face of his imposter syndrome. empowering him to stand taller in the face of his imposter syndrome.

Mark's primary therapeutic goals: overcoming his low self-esteem, and the fears of failure and success that had long plagued him. His determination remained steadfast as he diligently applied himself to the tasks at hand. His progress was steady, and the supportive presence of his fiancée continued to be a source of encouragement and a reminder of his focused personal strengths.

With each session, Mark's determination grew stronger, and his sense of self-worth began to flourish. The psychological skills he acquired enabled him to confront his fears and embrace a newfound confidence. No longer did he feel the need to pretend or diminish his achievements; Mark could finally take pride in his work and feel a sense of contentment. The presence of Mark's supportive fiancée provided a robust safety net, encouraging him to keep moving forward.

As Mark's therapy progressed, the roots of his anxiety and imposter syndrome were exposed. The psychiatrist delved into the formative experiences that shaped Mark's perceptions, helping him process and understand the origins of his struggles. By addressing these core issues, Mark's mental landscape began to shift, and he found himself better equipped to manage the challenges that lay ahead.

With each therapy session, Mark's determination grew stronger, and his newfound confidence permeated every aspect of his life, especially his work. The psychological cloud that had once hung over him lifted, and he could now appreciate his achievements without the crippling sense of inadequacy. His internal strength propelling him further along the path of healing. As Mark's therapy progressed, the roots of his anxiety were exposed, and he found himself better equipped to face the challenges that lay ahead, both personally and professionally.

THE SOCIAL MEDIA MANIA

Tina, an avid social media user, found herself increasingly engrossed in the virtual world. Her dedication to her online life was unwavering; she was forever connected, often neglecting her studies. It seemed as though every spare moment was devoted to the glow of her screen, messaging and engaging with her vast network of friends. Her virtual existence was a busy one, filled with constant notifications and conversations. It was a place where she felt increasingly at home, and real life often took a back seat to this engaging digital realm. Despite her academic workload, Tina's online presence remained a priority, and she would often rush through her schoolwork to make time for her virtual duties.

Tina's story unfolded as the college student's obsession with her digital life reached new heights. Her dedication to her online persona and the constant validation it brought was becoming a defining feature of her existence. Yet, amidst the excitement of her virtual world, a sense of unease began to settle in, as if the lines between her digital and real lives were beginning to blur.

Amidst Tina's seemingly fulfilling virtual life, a subtle shift occurred. The once-constant flow of messages and notifications began to wane, and Tina felt a sudden dichotomy as her digital friends started to lose interest. Unbeknownst to her, Tina had become a victim of her own success. Her appeal, which had initially drawn others in, seemed to intimidate her followers, creating a distance between them and her. Tina found herself perplexed and disoriented as the messages and interactions that once flooded her screen now trickled in sparingly.

The realization of this digital downfall left Tina feeling despondent and alone. As Tina scrolled endlessly, a sense of disconnection from her former online community intensified. She failed to see the parallel decline in her real-life connections, her obsession with the digital realm having diminished her relationships outside of it. The once solid foundation of her offline life now mirrored the volatility of her online existence.

Tina's digital world, once a realm of endless connections, began to unravel before her very eyes. Her online presence, once a hub of vibrant activity, started to falter, causing her to feel a profound sense of isolation. The messages and notifications that previously flooded her screen now dwindled to a trickle, leaving her perplexed and disoriented. Their virtual interactions with her, once engaging and frequent, now waned, leaving her desperate for connection.

Amidst this turmoil, Tina found herself increasingly detached from reality, stranded in a disorienting limbo between her two disparate lives. Her endless scrolling and quest for virtual validation became a desperate endeavor, as the interactions that once defined her online happiness were now scarce.

Tina's story is highlighting the delicate balance between digital connection and real-life fulfillment. As the lines between her worlds blurred, the need to reconnect with reality became imperative. Tina's digital bubble had burst, leaving her adrift in a sea of silence. Her online world, once a bustling hub of activity, had suddenly gone quiet, and the notifications that once brought her joy now lay dormant. As the messages dwindled, a sense of loneliness settled in, casting a shadow over her mood.

The decline went unnoticed at first, but as the days turned into weeks, the stark reality became evident. Tina found herself increasingly detached from her digital realm, a realm that had become her second home. Her once vibrant and fulfilling virtual life was now a distant memory, and the lack of interaction left her feeling aimless.

The endless scrolling and the desperate search for validation had become a hollow pursuit, and Tina's obsession had left her vulnerable. As she withdrew into herself, real life seemed to mirror the emptiness of her digital existence. The once vibrant college student, always engrossed in her devices, now walked the corridors with a somber step. The glow of her screen paled in comparison to the vibrant campus life that buzzed around her, yet she remained oblivious to the potential connections that lay beyond.

As Tina's obsession reached its apex, a strange dissonance set in. The blurring of her digital and real-life boundaries had created a strange dissonance, rendering her detached from the world around her. The once clear divide between her online and offline personas had disappeared, leaving her adrift in a disorienting limbo. Reconnecting with reality became an urgent task, a means to reclaim her life from the haunting shadows of a fading virtual realm.

Tina's digital life lay dormant, the buzz and bustle of her online existence replaced by an eerie silence. The lack of notifications and messages left her feeling adrift, a sense of loneliness permeating her being. As the days melded into weeks, the once vibrant social media enthusiast found herself increasingly alone and withdrawn.

The decline in Tina's online world went unnoticed by most, yet the consequences were profound. Her mood darkened as the gloom of depression settled in, stealing her motivation and energy. The once diligent college student now struggled to rise from her bed, the allure of the virtual world dimmed to a faint glimmer. Tina sank deeper into her dire loss and the emptiness of her online realm.

Amidst this somber turn of events, a concerned classmate, Jane, took notice of Tina's waning presence on campus. Her absence from lectures and her general air of despondency didn't go unnoticed. Jane, ever the empathetic soul, felt compelled to act, aware of the delicate balance between online and real-life interactions. With discretion, she reached out, aiming to bridge the widening gap between Tina's worlds.

Jane noticed Tina's distant behavior and reached out, but her attempts at connection were met with radio silence. Tina's absorption in her digital world had reached a new peak, leaving little room for real-life interactions, including her relationship with her boyfriend, George, which she had recently ended.

Jane's concern grew as Tina's absence from campus life became more pronounced, her mood increasingly despondent. Tina's once vibrant social media presence had grown stale, its allure faded. The endless scroll and pursuit of virtual approval had left her feeling hollow. As she withdrew further into herself, her online world became a ghost town, its silence echoing loudly.

Unbeknownst to Jane, Tina's descent into her digital realm had created a chasm between them, one that Jane was determined to bridge. Jane's empathy urged her to persist despite Tina's initial brush-offs. She knew the value of their connection and the delicate balance between online and offline life all too well. There was a time when they had shared many memories and experiences, and Jane was convinced that Tina's return to the real world was only a matter of time. But that time seemed uncertain, as Tina was deeply entrenched in her digital bubble, oblivious to the warmth of human connection that Jane sought to restore.

Tina's descent into the digital abyss continued unabated as the world around her faded into obscurity. Her once vibrant existence had transformed into a somber shell, consumed by the endless scroll of her social media addiction. As the days melded into a grinding routine, the decline in her online popularity went unnoticed. The notifications that once lit up her world like fireworks now lay dormant, leaving a gaping void in their absence. The campus corridors echoed with the melancholy of Tina's footsteps as she withdrew further into her solitary self. Her mood, a dark cloud hanging over her, went unnoticed.

Tina's loneliness reached unprecedented depths; her despair knew no bounds. The allure of the virtual world had lost its sparkle, yet she found herself unable to extricate herself from its grasp. A sense of hopelessness enveloped her, leading her to contemplate the unthinkable. In the stillness of her darkest moments, a plan began to form, a last resort to end the pain that felt like an inescapable prison. Unbeknownst to Jane, Tina's descent had reached its final stages, and the clock ticked towards a potential tragedy.

Concern turned to alarm as Tina's absence from lectures and general despondency grew. Tina's digital bubble remained impenetrable, a fortress guarding her from the reality that threatened to engulf her. Unbeknownst to Jane, Tina's descent into the abyss of her making was irreversible, a tragic end to a story that unfolded in silence.

One fateful night, Jane's worries proved well-founded. An ominous hush fell as Tina's lifeless body was discovered, a victim of her own despair. The lines between her virtual and real lives had blurred, and the consequences were almost fatal.

The mystery surrounding Tina's declining mental and physical health deepened as the days went by. Jane arrived to a chilling discovery—an attempted overdose, a desperate cry for help that went unnoticed by all but Jane. With alarm bells ringing, Jane took immediate action. She called the authorities, who responded swiftly, finding Tina unconscious and administering the necessary medical aid. Time seemed to stand still as they fought to stabilize her condition. The world held its breath, awaiting news of Tina's fate, while Jane stood by, haunted by guilt thoughts that she might have done more.

The enigmatic figure of Tina loomed in the emergency room, her body motionless save for the rise and fall of her chest, aided by a respirator. The circumstances that brought her here remained a mystery to all but one. Jane, her concerned classmate, stood vigil, haunted by the possibility of what might have been if she hadn't acted on her alarm.

Tina's world had collapsed inwards, a slow descent into the abyss of depression and despair. Her online realm, once a vibrant sanctuary, had become a ghostly shell of its former self, the notifications and messages that once brought her joy now a distant memory. As her digital connections faded, so too did her will to persist, leading her down a dark path to an attempted exit.

The hospital's intense atmosphere was permeated with an air of tension as doctors fought to stabilize Tina's critical condition. Time seemed suspended in the tense silence, broken only by the beeping monitors and the hushed voices of the medical staff. Jane's eyes never left her friend's motionless form, a stark reminder of the delicate balance between virtual and real-life connections.

Days passed, and Tina lay motionless in the intensive care unit, her eyes closed, unaware of the world around her. The bustling hospital room fell silent as the minutes ticked by, and the patients shared a collective sense of uncertainty, their gazes fixed upon the motionless form of the young woman.

Jane, her loyal classmate and confidant, kept a vigilant watch by Tina's bedside, never leaving her side during her stay in the hospital. The concerned looks on the faces of the medical staff reflected the gravity of Tina's condition, as they attended to her with meticulous care. The atmosphere was heavy with anticipation, as if the room itself held its breath, awaiting the moment when Tina would either open her eyes or slip further away. The silence was broken only by the soft beeping of machines and the occasional hushed conversation between the medical professionals.

Jane's eyes, filled with anxiety and hope, never wavered from her friend's face, as she silently wills Tina to pull through. Outside the hospital room, the sun set, casting a golden hue through the large windows, a gentle reminder of the world awaiting Tina's return.

Tina lay motionless in the sterile environment of the intensive care unit, her eyes closed. The young woman remained in a world of her own, her online realm a distant memory. The hospital's hushed corridors and the somber faces of the medical staff reflected the gravity of her condition.

Then, amidst the stillness, a shift occurred. Tina's eyes slowly opened, and the world rushed back into focus. Her gaze landed on Jane, a powerful reminder of their deep connection, and a glimmer of hope ignited within her. Jane's presence, a constant in Tina's recovery, seemed to reassure her that she was not alone. The walls of her digital fortress began to crumble, as the reality of her situation and the depth of her friendship with Jane slowly sank in.

The psychiatrist found himself drawn into the enigmatic world of Tina's experiences as he delved deeper into her attempt at taking her own life. Her descent into the digital realm had been a solitary one, a gradual withdrawal from reality that few had noticed until it was almost too late. The story of her decline unfolded amidst a sea of screens and notifications, a tragic tale of obsession and its consequences.

The psychiatrist uncovered the depths of Tina's depression, the relentless symptoms of clinical depression that had haunted her for so long. The virtual world had become her refuge, a place where she sought validation and escape. But it was a treacherous realm, one that could just as easily consume and isolate its denizens. As Tina's online presence waned, so too did her connection with the real world, leading her down a dark path of despair.

With each revelation, the psychiatrist painted a clearer picture of Tina's descent, the blurring boundaries between her digital and physical existence. He learned of the gradual disintegration of her relationships and her increasing sense of loneliness. The virtual bubble she had created around herself had hidden the depth of her despair from all but a few, the silent screams for help going unnoticed until Jane's timely intervention. Now, as Tina lay recovering in the hospital, the psychiatrist aimed to unravel the mysteries of her mind, leading her towards a path of healing and self-discovery.

Tina's condition remained critical as she lay motionless in the Intensive Care Unit. The weight of her depression and isolation was evident, a deep chasm that threatened to swallow her whole. Yet, amidst the gloom, a flicker of hope ignited. Her close friend Jane, ever vigilant, brought a bouquet of vibrant flowers, a subtle gesture packed with meaning.

The flowers, a vibrant assortment of colors, reflected a determined attempt to brighten Tina's somber world. Jane's unwavering support, a constant in Tina's recovery, offered a glimmer of light that infiltrated the dark clouds hanging over her. As she lay weak and vulnerable, the gesture touched her deeply, stirring a subtle shift within.

The hospital room, usually a bustling hub of activity, fell silent as the medical staff paused to witness the exchange. The power of friendship, a silent yet potent force, permeated the air, offering a sliver of hope amidst the uncertainty. Tina's journey towards healing had begun, a slow crawl back from the brink, guided by the unwavering support of Jane's friendship.

As time progressed, the psychiatrist delved further into the enigma that was Tina's attempt at taking her own life. Her descent into the digital abyss had been a slow and insidious one. As the story of her fall unfolded, a picture emerged of a young woman lost in a world that had ultimately consumed her.

Tina's online life, once a vibrant tapestry of connections, had gradually unraveled, leaving her feeling completely isolated and alone. The psychiatrist's objective gaze uncovered the depths of Tina's depression, the relentless onslaught of symptoms that had accompanied her for so long, and the virtual realm that had both soothed and exacerbated her pain. The lines between her digital and physical selves had blurred, leading to a steady descent into total darkness. Yet, amidst this gloom, there remains a glimmer of hope.

Tina's recovery continued under the watchful eye of the psychiatrist and the unwavering support of Jane. The powerful effects of the medication combined with the tranquil atmosphere of the hospital grounds, where the pair often walked, gradually rekindled their friendship. Tina, weak but determined, confessed her fears to Jane one day, expressing her belief that she had lost her friend forever.

Jane reassured her that their bond remained unbreakable, a sentiment that ignited a spark of hope within Tina's heart. The psychiatrist made progress in understanding Tina's descent into the digital abyss. Her story unfolded against a backdrop of screens and notifications, a tragic spiral of obsession that isolated her from the real world. As her online presence waned, so too did her connections with those around her, leading to the dark depths of despair. The intervention had arrived just in time, offering a chance at recovery and a reunion with reality.

The hospital's serene surroundings provided a much-needed sanctuary as Tina and Jane spent increasing amounts of time together. Their bond, strengthened by shared experiences, grew deeper with each passing day. The psychiatrist's insights, combined with the pair's collective efforts, painted a clearer picture of Tina's journey towards healing. The enigma of her attempted suicide and the role of her digital world slowly unraveled, revealing a cautionary tale of the dangers that lurked within the seemingly innocent realm of social media.

The psychiatrist explained at the world of social media may hold an enigmatic allure that ensnares its users, luring them into a false sense of belonging. Tina, an avid user, found herself increasingly entangled in this virtual web, where the boundaries between reality and the online realm blurred. As her obsession deepened, her true life began to wither, a sad spectator to her digital existence.

The bustling campus, once a hub of activity and camaraderie, now echoed with the melancholy of Tina's solitary presence. Her fixation on the screen's glow pushed away real-life connections, rendering them obsolete. The more engaged she became in this virtual world, the more the lines blurred, and a disorienting dissonance set in.

Unbeknownst to Tina, her descent was being closely observed by a concerned friend and classmate, Jane. She noticed the gradual transformation of Tina's behavior, her absence from reality, and the somber air that surrounded her. Jane's empathy urged her to act, but Tina's absorption became absolute, leaving little opportunity for a real-life breakthrough. As Tina's digital world crumbled around her, Jane's efforts became a desperate cry against the encroaching darkness.

The lessons learned in continued therapy remained at the forefront of Tina's mind, guiding her toward a newfound confidence. Her insecurities, though not entirely extinguished, no longer held the same power over her decisions. The world of social media, though tempting, now held less sway over Tina's life.

Tina recognized the importance of balancing her virtual and real-life interactions, embracing the latter with open arms. Her journey, though fraught with challenges, had equipped her with the wisdom to navigate the complexities of both realms.

The campus corridors echoed with the laughter of her newfound joy as Tina discovered the enduring power of the real world. Meanwhile, the psychiatrist continued to unravel the mysteries of the digital realm's influence on the human psyche, using Tina's experience as a cautionary tale, one that emphasized the importance of real-world connections and the potential dangers that lurked within the seemingly innocent realm of social media.

THE CAR ACCIDENT

One early morning, Anne continued her journey to work, unaware of the impending disaster about to unfold. As she approached the bustling intersection of Fifth street and Main, her vehicle was suddenly thrust into chaos. A speeding car, running a red light, collided with Anne's car, sending it into a deadly spin. The impact flung Anne's car to the side, pirouetting off into the distance before crashing into a streetlight with a jarring finality. The force of the collision threw Anne against her seatbelt, rendering her unconscious.

Meanwhile, the culprit's vehicle sped off into the morning haze, leaving Anne injured and alone amidst the wreckage. Fortunately, help was close at hand. Within minutes, the shrill sirens of an ambulance echoed through the air, and EMS workers sprang into action. They found Anne slumped over the steering wheel, dazed and disoriented, her injuries a testament to the violent encounter.

The emergency department buzzed with activity as Anne was rushed in, her condition causing great concern. The medical team swiftly attended to her, assessing her injuries and stabilizing her vital signs. Anne's injuries were extensive, with multiple fractures and a severe concussion leaving her vulnerable and immobile. As Anne fought for consciousness, the medical professionals fought their own battle to save her, every second counting towards her recovery.

The car accident had a profound impact on Anne's life, leaving her physically and mentally battered. Her recovery was a slow and painful process, both physically and emotionally. Despite the excellent care she received at the hospital, the memory of the traumatic event lingered, manifesting as anxiety and depressing thoughts.

The once vibrant and energetic Anne found herself withdrawn and isolated, struggling to find joy in activities that once brought her pleasure. As time moved relentlessly forward, Anne's physical wounds began to heal, but the psychological scars ran deep. Nightmares and flashbacks haunted her sleep, and her thoughts often wandered to the fateful morning of the accident.

The loss of her vitality and strength left her feeling vulnerable and helpless. She found herself unable to return to work, and the very mention of the incident ignited a flame of fear within her. Several weeks passed, and Anne's condition remained fragile. She relied heavily on the support of her sister, Amanda, who had become a constant support during her recovery.

The car accident had however left Anne's life in tatters, her once-vibrant existence replaced by a cloud of anxiety and despair. The physical pain of her injuries was constant, a stark reminder of the traumatic event. Her days continued to be filled with grim memories, nightmares, and flashbacks of the violent collision. The mental scars ran deep, affecting her psyche and leaving her emotionally battered.

Anne's withdrawal from the world continued, her once bubbly personality now a distant memory. The simple mention of the accident sent shivers down her spine, triggering intense fear and a sense of powerlessness. The vibrant and energetic woman had transformed into a shadow of her former self, struggling to find joy and unable to return to work.

Her sister, Amanda, became a constant source of support and comfort during this dark period. Several weeks passed, and while Anne's physical injuries were healing, her psychological recovery remained stagnant. The anxiety and depression intensified, keeping her confined to the confines of her home. The thought of stepping back into the real world elicited an overwhelming sense of fear, as if the accident had left an indelible mark on her very being.

Yet, amidst the gloom, a glimmer of hope emerged. Anne found solace in the little things—a warm smile from Amanda, the soothing warmth of a sunny day, and the gentle breeze carrying the scent of spring. These moments offered a fleeting reprieve from the incessant painful memories.

As the days turned into weeks, Anne's psychological recovery stagnated. While her physical injuries were healing, the scars on her psyche ran deeper, resistant to the soothing touch of time. As much as her sister, Amanda, tried to uplift her spirits, Anne's emotional injuries were entering a deeper depression.

Anne would spend hours in bed, staring at the walls, feeling the weight of loneliness press down on her. The darkness intensified when Amanda was absent, leaving her alone with her thoughts, which invariably wandered down the path of despair. There was a persistent ache in Anne's soul, a dull throb that nothing seemed to alleviate. The accident had left an indelible mark, a shadow that followed her every step.

The psychiatrist delved into Anne's psychological state, unearthing the remnants of a past trauma. Anne, it seemed, had been a victim of a traumatic bicycle accident during her college years. The memory of that fateful event had remained etched in her mind, leaving her with a lingering fear of both bicycles and driving.

The psychiatrist uncovered the profound impact of this accident, a hidden wound that had reopened with the recent car crash. As the psychiatrist continued his inquiry, Anne revealed the profound effects the bicycle accident had on her life. She described the long recovery process and the persistent fear that had plagued her ever since. The thought of getting behind the wheel induced a sense of panic, but Anne had bravely forced herself to drive to support her working life.

Now, the recent car accident had rekindled the old trauma, and the psychological scars reopened, leaving her more vulnerable than ever. Recognizing the severity of Anne's condition, the psychiatrist devised a comprehensive treatment plan. He emphasized the importance of processing and overcoming the trauma of her past accidents.

Anne's journey towards healing had begun, but it would be a challenging road ahead. The psychiatrist equipped her with an array of coping mechanisms and therapeutic tools to navigate the complex aftermath of these dual traumas. The first steps were taken towards embarking into recovery, guided by the psychiatrist's expertise and Anne's unwavering determination.

The psychiatrist's expert guidance became a beacon of hope amidst Anne's darkening storms. He crafted a careful treatment plan, tailored to help Anne confront and process the trauma of her past mishaps. It was a slow and challenging journey, but with each session, Anne found herself better equipped to face her fears.

The psychiatrist's approach was multifaceted, incorporating an array of therapeutic techniques. He encouraged Anne to confront her anxiety head-on by gradually exposing her to the very situations that triggered her fear. It was a daunting task, but with Anne's determination and the psychiatrist's support, she took small yet significant steps towards recovery.

As Anne continued her sessions, the psychiatrist delved deeper into the enigma of her mental struggles. He unraveled the intricate web of Anne's thoughts, helping her dispel the clouds of doubt and despair that had consumed her. With each revelation, Anne's perspective shifted, and the world around her came back into focus.

The exploration of Anne's past accidents and their lingering effects was just one aspect of her therapy. The psychiatrist also aided Anne in exploring the roots of her anxiety, often probing into her family history and childhood experiences. It was a delicate journey, one that unearthed long-forgotten memories and emotions. Yet, with each recollection, Anne felt a sense of release, like a weight was being lifted from her shoulders.

As the sessions progressed, Anne's determination grew stronger. The psychological insights she gained empowered her, fostering a newfound sense of confidence. With each small step, her appetite for life returned, and the psychiatrist's goal of helping Anne reclaim her true self seemed within reach.

Yet, the road to full recovery was never a straight one. Anne faced relapses and setbacks, moments where the trauma seemed to overwhelm her progress. During these trying times, the psychiatrist's presence became a beacon of stability, guiding her back towards the path of healing. As the chapters of Anne's story unfolded, the psychiatrist found himself captivated by the resilience of the human spirit. Anne's journey, though fraught with difficulty, showcased the incredible strength that lies within us.

Her progress became a testament to the power of the human will and the potential for growth amidst adversity. The end of each session marked a new beginning, a chance for Anne to integrate the lessons learned into her everyday life. The psychiatrist's words resonated within her, encouraging a newfound sense of exploration.

She discovered a world beyond her trauma, embracing hobbies and experiences that brought her joy. Anne's progress was a testament to her dedication and strength. Her journey was a change towards of hope and determination, a tale of the human capacity for recovery.

Anne's journey of healing continued as she discovered a newfound passion for gardening. With her sister Amanda, she meticulously planted a vibrant garden, a colorful tapestry of perennials, sunflowers, marigolds, coneflowers, lilies, and other flowering plants. The physical act of tending to nature brought a sense of calm and purpose to Anne's life, offering a welcome distraction from her traumatic past.

As the seeds grew into sturdy plants, so too did Anne's determination to overcome the shadows of her recent accident. Each day, Anne found solace in the simple joy of tending to her garden. The process became a therapeutic ritual, a silent meditation that soothed her troubled mind. The vibrant blooms became a tangible symbol of hope and resilience, a reminder of the beauty that could arise from the darkness.

Amidst the fragrant flowers, Anne found a sense of peace, and the memories of the car crash faded slightly, like a bad dream that was slowly dissipating. The garden became a sanctuary for Anne, a place where the weight of her struggles momentarily lifted. Time spent with Amanda in this peaceful oasis fostered a deeper connection between the sisters. Their shared love for the natural world became a bonding experience, weaving a new layer into their already unbreakable bond. Together, they watched the garden grow, a living testament to the cycle of life and the enduring power of nature.

As Anne continued her sessions with the psychiatrist, she found solace in sharing her progress in the garden. The psychiatrist incorporated this new development into their sessions, understanding the positive influence it had on Anne's mental health. Together, they explored the calming effects of her newfound hobby and how it helped her manage the anxiety triggered by the car accident.

Anne's determination to overcome her struggles grew stronger with each day. The garden became a symbol of hope and resilience, a tangible reminder that beauty could arise from the depths of despair. She took pride in tending to her plants, finding a sense of accomplishment and joy in their growth and vibrant colors.

The garden's peaceful atmosphere became a safe haven, allowing Anne to confront her fears and embrace a newfound sense of freedom. Each session with the psychiatrist brought new insights and a deeper understanding of herself, helping her navigate the complexities of her recovery.

Anne's recovery progressed steadily as she continued to work from home, finding solace in the comfort of a familiar environment. The additional time at home allowed her to focus on her rehabilitation, both physically and mentally. She found a new appreciation for the little things, like taking a leisurely drive when the roads were clear and presenting her friends with the flowers from her garden.

Her sister, Amanda, remained a constant source of support, often joining Anne on these therapeutic drives. The fresh air and vibrant scenery provided a welcome change of pace from the four walls of their home. Anne felt a sense of freedom as she sat behind the wheel, a symbol of her gradual return to a life of independence.

As Anne's condition improved, she became increasingly interested in helping others. She reached out to friends who had also experienced trauma, offering support and guidance born from her own trials. She shared her story, providing a much-needed shoulder to lean on, and in return, she received a newfound sense of purpose. This mutual support system became a powerful tool in her recovery,

Outside, the sun shone brightly on a crisp morning as Anne and Amanda embarked on a special journey. They drove to the local nursery, a place brimming with life and color. Anne had found solace in gardening, and today was a special day as they set out to purchase new plants to enhance her healing sanctuary. The sisters carefully selected an assortment of vibrant blooms, each with its unique meaning and purpose.

The drive home was filled with lively conversation and

excitement as Anne and Amanda imagined the garden's new possibilities. Upon arrival, they swiftly got to work, tend to their new plants with gentle care. As they dug into the earth, a sense of calm washed over Anne. The physical exertion and connection with nature served as a potent remedy, easing the pain and anxiety that had held her captive for so long. The new plants added a splash of color to the garden, each one a visual reminder of Anne's progress and resilience.

The vibrant hues reflected her determination, and the fragrant blooms brought a sense of peace. Anne found purpose in her green thumb, a new hobby that helped her manage the aftermath of the car accident. As the sun set on another fulfilling day, Anne felt a sense of accomplishment, and the garden glowed with the promise of tomorrow.

Anne's progress became a beacon, illuminating the challenging path of mental health recovery. And so, the story of Anne's healing continued, a narrative of courage and resilience, guided by the light of professional expertise and the indomitable human spirit.

Anne's progress became a beacon, illuminating the challenging path of mental health recovery. And so, the story of Anne's healing continued, a narrative of courage and resilience, guided by the light of professional expertise and the indomitable human spirit.

THE NEW PASSION

Bob's life had taken an unexpected turn after the retail store he managed for a decade underwent a significant downsizing. He found himself among the employees who were let go, receiving a meager severance package. As he navigated the complexities of unemployment, Bob sought solace in the company of his family, his spouse Jessica, a stay-at-home mom, and their two young children.

Bob stood shell-shocked amidst the ruins of his once-stable world. The news of his dismissal on his 45th birthday had sent his life into a tailspin, evoking memories of a past marked by economic turbulence and prolonged unemployment. The severance package provided a temporary crutch, but Bob's thoughts raced towards the uncertain future ahead. As he reflected on the chaotic situation, his spouse, Jessica, a steadfast stay-at-home mom, and their two young children became the beacon of light in his hour of darkness.

He found some solace in their company, Yet, the shadow of his birthday dismissal lingered, prompting Bob to confront the demons of his past. He recalled the lengthy unemployment spell that had plagued him, forcing him to move back in with his parents until this recent retail job came his way. Now, faced with another bout of uncertainty, Bob's determination ignited.

He found solace in their innocent faces, unaware of the turmoil that had befallen their lives. But the weight of his birthday dismissal lingered, a constant reminder of the economic turbulence and prolonged unemployment he had faced in his past. The memory of those challenging times sent a chill down Bob's spine. He had been forced to move back in with his parents after losing his previous job. Their well-meaning but smothering presence had made his job search a tedious ordeal. Eventually, he found himself packing his bags once more, seeking refuge with a compassionate friend who offered him a place to stay. The stress and depression he experienced during that period remained etched in his memory.

The weight of his situation lingered, an ever-present reminder of the challenges ahead. Bob's feelings of disappointment and discouragement weighed heavily on him following the recent downturn in sales at the store. He couldn't help but blame himself for the decline, especially after a disgruntled employee was caught stealing, which seemed to coincide with the drop in foot traffic. Bob reflected on the impact this would have on his family.

Bob stood in the midst of an unfamiliar landscape; his world turned upside down. The severance package seemed a meager band-aid on a gaping wound. As the reality of his situation sank in, Bob felt a familiar sense of despair creep up. The memories of his previous unemployment, and the subsequent strain on his mental health, surfaced like unwelcome ghosts.

The thought of facing another prolonged stint without work triggered a sense of powerlessness. Bob's anxiety intensified, clouding his judgment and fueling his depression. He withdrew into himself, finding solace only in the company of his spouse, Jessica, and their young family. Their innocent faces were a fleeting reminder of the innocence he once knew, a time before the weight of financial instability had borne down on him.

The weight of his circumstances was a relentless force. Bob's sleep was disturbed, his appetite waned, and the very thought of another job search discouraged and exhausted him. The stress manifested physically, mentally, and emotionally. Jessica's unwavering support was a constant in Bob's sea of uncertainty.

One day Jessica provided a glimmer of hope, encouraging him to seek professional help. Understanding the gravity of Bob's situation, she reached out to her father for financial assistance, ensuring the household's ongoing needs were met.

Bob's journey towards healing began with the support of a compassionate psychiatrist. The psychiatrist's objective approach helped Bob confront the demons of his past, unpacking the psychological baggage that had weighed him down. With each session, Bob regained a sense of hope and the courage to face the working world anew. The psychiatrist equipped him with tools to challenge his negative thought patterns, empowering him to stand tall in the face of adversity.

The weight of Bob's past loomed large, a haunting reminder of the economic storms he had weathered. The memory of prolonged unemployment, and the strain it had placed on his mental health, surfaced like a nasty wound. The thought of returning to those dark days sent shivers down his spine, recalling the time he had sought refuge with his parents, and later, with a compassionate friend.

Amidst this chaos, Bob discovered a glimmer of hope. His cousin had just opened a new pizza parlor and required a manager. Bob seized this opportunity with both hands, embracing the prospect of a fresh start. He threw himself into this new endeavor, finding particular joy in serving the enthusiastic children who flocked to the pizza parlor. A slow smile of satisfaction would spread across his face as he watched the delight on their young faces.

Each day, Bob's determination grew stronger. He relished the challenge of learning the intricacies of this new trade, finding purpose and meaning in the bustling kitchen. The stress of his previous life began to lift, and a renewed sense of hope blossomed in its place. Bob's journey towards healing had begun, guided by the comforting presence of family and the excitement of a brand-new passion.

As Bob settled into his new role, he began to visualize a different kind of future. The pizza parlor buzzed with activity, becoming a sanctuary where he could escape the demons of his past. His cousin provided him with the freedom to innovate, and Bob thrived in this environment, creating new pizza recipes that became firm favorites with the local clientele.

Bob's renewed strength and purpose had a profound effect on his overall well-being. The clouds of anxiety and depression that had loomed over him began to disperse, and a sense of clarity emerged. He found himself more present for his family, reveling in the simple pleasures of sharing mealtimes and engaging in the children's playful antics.

Bob's journey towards healing and self-discovery continued as he found renewed energy and purpose in his work at the pizza parlor. With each passing day, the world seemed to brighten, and the clouds of anxiety that had once loomed over him began to scatter. The prospect of feeding people delicious, freshly made pizzas brought a sense of satisfaction and joy to Bob.

Bob's cousin's new enterprise buzzed with activity. The pizza parlors become a new sanctuary for Bob, allowing him to immerse himself in the art of pizza-making. The freedom to experiment and innovate excited him, and he relished the prospect of creating new recipes.

The local clientele grew fond of Bob's specialities, particularly the pizza quattro formaggi, a four-cheese masterpiece that became a menu favorite. As the pizzeria's popularity grew, Bob's confidence strengthened. He found purpose and meaning in his work. With each pizza he crafted, Bob felt a surge of enthusiasm.

The prospect of managing and shaping another successful enterprise appealed to him, and he shared his vision with his cousin. The cousin, impressed by Bob's passion and determination, decided to take the leap of faith. Recognizing the potential in Bob's ambitions, they pooled their resources for a new culinary frontier. Bob's leadership skills were put to the test as he oversaw the creation of a new pizzeria, applying the lessons learned from his previous success.

The new establishment mirrored the prosperity of its predecessor, drawing in a crowd of eager customers. Bob's dedication knew no bounds as he oversaw the seamless operation, ensuring every aspect ran smoothly. The staff adored him, recognizing his fair and supportive leadership, and the customers praised his culinary creations. As the pizzerias flourished, Bob's financial stability improved, allowing him to repay Jessica's father for his kindness.

The sense of accomplishment and financial security lifted a weight from Bob's shoulders, and he found himself breathing easier than he had in years. The world had become a brighter place, and Bob knew that despite the storms he had weathered, the sunshine of success could always break through the clouds.

Life for Bob was far from perfect, yet he felt a newfound sense of control and hope. He still attended sessions with the psychiatrist, processing the psychological fallout of his unemployment and finding solace in the understanding and tools they provided. With each passing day, Bob's story became one of resilience and rebirth, a testament to the power of the human spirit.

THE TALL BRIDGE

The tall bridge echoed with the sound of a few chirping craws as Jennifer stood on the ledge, her eyes fixed on the bustling city below. The 30-year-old executive's hands gripped the railing, a barrier between life and death, as she wrestled with the demons in her mind. The dark winter day mirrored the gloom in her soul, a soul tired of fighting the never-ending battle against hopelessness. Her grip tightened as she contemplated ending it all, the weight of rejection from her long-term boyfriend, who had left her for another woman, pushing her to the edge. The police were alerted to Jennifer's presence on the bridge, their sirens blaring as they raced against time to save her. The cameras installed on the bridge had detected her perilous stance, and now, against the backdrop of rushing vehicles and somber skies, an intense struggle between life and death unfolded. Jennifer's fingers trembled, her breath forming small clouds of despair in the cold winter air. The police worked swiftly, establishing a perimeter to ensure Jennifer's safety and provide her the space she needed to confront her inner demons. The police, experienced in such situations, approached with caution, aware that one wrong move could push Jennifer further away from salvation.

The tall bridge echoed with the mournful cries of crows, their ominous calls adding to the gloom of the dark winter day. Jennifer stood on the ledge, her eyes fixed on the dreary deep river below, a stark contrast to the bustling city life that continued unaware of the drama unfolding. Officer Brittany, experienced in these situations, approached Jennifer with caution, her warm and reassuring presence offering a glimmer of hope amidst the despair.

As Jennifer stood on the edge of the tall bridge, her eyes fixed on the dark water below, Officer Brittany approached with caution. "Are you Jennifer?" she asked softly, but received no response. Jennifer's face was ashen, a stark contrast to the bustling activity behind her. Brittany, experienced in these situations, remained composed. "My name is Brittany, and I'm here to help you. I have a warm blanket to keep you comfortable." She hoped the gesture would help break the ice and create an opportunity for dialogue. Jennifer's trembling fingers tightened around the railing, the cold winter air doing little to ease her despair. The police had arrived swiftly, their sirens blaring, and now a tense standoff ensued. "I want you to know that we're here for you," Brittany continued, her voice warm and reassuring. "We can work through this together. You don't have to face this alone." The officer's empathy seemed to break through the thick wall of Jennifer's despair. A flicker of hope ignited within her eyes. As Jennifer stepped back from the ledge, the weight of the world seemed to lift from her shoulders.

Brittany's calm and collected demeanor seemed to pierce through the thick fog of Jennifer's depression. She extended her arm, a warm blanket, a simple gesture that helped break the ice. "My name is Brittany, and I'm here to help you," she assured, her voice melting the icy barrier that had enclosed Jennifer's heart. The officer's empathy and understanding seemed to spark a flicker of life within Jennifer's soul, and she slowly unwound her white knuckled grip from the railing. As Jennifer took a tentative step back from the ledge, a palpable sense of relief washed over her. The weight of the world, until now pressing down on her shoulders, lifted, and she allowed herself to be guided towards safety. Yet, the battle was not won.

The deep wells of depression ran deep within Jennifer, and she knew that her salvation lay not in the fleeting comfort of the moment but in the thorough evaluation and treatment that awaited her at the psychiatric emergency department. As she made her way there, she found solace in the thought that help was at hand, and perhaps, finally, the clouds of darkness would untangle.

The psychiatrist delved deep into Jennifer's psyche, unravelling the mysteries behind her suicidal attempt. It was a tragic tale of deep, hopeless depression; a dark cloud that had been building up for years, fueled by a sense of worthlessness and loneliness. The recent rejection by her long-term boyfriend, who had left her for another woman, had been the final straw. Jennifer's descent into despair had been a slow burn, her emotional pain going unnoticed by those around her. It was only when Officer Brittany, with her warm and reassuring presence, offered a glimmer of hope, that Jennifer took a step back from the ledge, and the weight of her world lifted. But the battle against depression was far from over. Jennifer's admission to the psychiatric emergency department marked the beginning of her road to recovery. The psychiatrist's expert evaluation revealed a complex web of intricate feelings—a poisonous thought process that had consumed her for so long.

The psychiatrist worked to unravel the cycles of despair, giving Jennifer the tools to challenge her damaging thoughts. It was a challenging journey, but one that offered her a glimmer of hope— a chance to reclaim her life and find meaning amidst the darkness.

The battle against depression was a formidable one. With the expert guidance of the psychiatrist, Jennifer embarked on a challenging journey of self-discovery. The psychiatrist equipped her with the weaponry to challenge the poisonous thought processes that had consumed her, offering a glimmer of hope for a life reclaimed.

The psychiatric emergency department buzzed with activity as Jennifer's case unfolded before the adept psychiatrist. It was a tragic narrative, a slow descent into despair fueled by a sense of loneliness and profound hopelessness. The recent breakup, marked by her boyfriend's infidelity, had been the catalyst.

Yet, underlying this was a intricate web of intricate emotions —a poisonous thought spiral that had consumed her for some extended time.

The psychiatrist delved deeper, unearthing the roots of Jennifer's anguish. With each revelation, a new layer of the onion was peeled back, exposing the depths of her anguish. Together, they worked to unravel the complex cycles of her despair, equipping her with the tools to challenge the detrimental thought patterns that had held her captive. It was a challenging journey, but one that held the promise of liberation.

Desiree, Jennifer's older sister, had arrived to offer her support, her concerns about Jennifer's mental health validated by the unfolding events. She had witnessed the tumultuous relationship and the telltale signs of Jennifer's boyfriend's toxicity. Now, she stood by her sister's side, a beacon of unwavering caring and determination, as Jennifer embarked on her recovery journey. The battle against the dark shadows of the mind was a formidable one, but with the psychiatrist's expertise and Desiree's steadfast companionship, there was a glimmer of hope for a life reborn.

The sisterly bond strengthened Jennifer's resolve, and she found solace in Desiree's unwavering commitment. The psychiatrist's insights equipped Jennifer to challenge the demons that had plagued her, and with each session, the clouds of depression lifted a little more. As Jennifer's perspective shifted, the world around her came into focus, offering a new hope.

The journey ahead promised to be circuitous, with setbacks and relapses along the way. Yet, Jennifer's determination burned brightly, and the psychiatrist's objective guidance provided a steadfast compass. Jennifer was admitted to the hospital's mental health unit.

The unit buzzed with activity as Jennifer's journey unfolded. It was a slow descent into despair, fueled by feelings of loneliness and the weight of an intricate web of thoughts. The psychiatrist met with Jennifer regularly and delved deeper, peeling back the layers of Jennifer's anguish, and equipped her with the tools to challenge these detrimental patterns. They explored the roots of her anguish, uncovering the formative experiences that shaped her perceptions. With each session, Jennifer's determination grew stronger, and the clouds of depression lifted a little higher.

The battle against mental illness was a formidable one, but Jennifer's resolve remained steadfast. With the support of her sister Desiree and the expertise of the psychiatrist, there was a promising glimmer of hope for a life of recovery and renewed purpose. As Jennifer's perspective shifted, the world around her came into focus, offering a new hope and a future to look forward to. Yet, it was a road filled with twists and turns, and Jennifer prepared herself for the challenges ahead.

As Jennifer continued her battle with the dark clouds of depression, the psychiatrist recommended a customized treatment plan, which included administering an antidepressant to alleviate her symptoms. The medication gradually began to take effect, lifting the heavy veil of gloom from Jennifer's mind. Her appetite returned, and with it, a renewed sense of energy and hope.

With each passing day, Jennifer felt a gradual shift. The weight of the world lifted from her shoulders, and a newfound sense of determination ignited within her. She found purpose in the little things, a simple smile, or a ray of winter sun breaking through the clouds. The prospect of a brighter future began to take root in her mind, offering a compelling reason to fight for life.

The psychiatrist's expert guidance remained a constant in Jennifer's recovery journey. Their sessions together delved into the intricate web of thoughts that had consumed her, providing her with the tools to challenge and rewrite the poisonous narratives that had held her back. It was a slow and arduous journey, but with each small victory, Jennifer's confidence grew stronger.

As Jennifer's perspective shifted, the world around her transformed. She began to see a glimmer of light in the bustling city that had once seemed so dreary. The psychiatrist's unwavering support, coupled with the love and dedication of her sister Desiree, created a powerful trio, a beacon of hope amidst the storm.

Together, they faced the challenges that lay ahead, prepared for the twists and turns of the road to recovery. Jennifer's determination remained steadfast, and the clouds of depression lifted further with each new day. The battle was not yet won, but Jennifer's progress ignited a flame of hope, a promise of a life reborn from the ashes of despair.

Jennifer's journey of healing continued as she found solace in the artistic talents she had always possessed. Desiree, her supportive sister, had provided her with a new perspective, encouraging her to explore the world of drawing and oil painting. Their walks in the park nearby had become a sanctuary, a peaceful escape from the chaos that had consumed Jennifer's life.

The sisterly bond strengthened Jennifer's resolve, and their conversations meandered into the realm of possibilities for Jennifer's future. Desiree offered to host Jennifer at her home, a welcoming environment where she could focus on her passion and regain her footing. The art studio in Desiree's home became Jennifer's creative sanctuary, a place where she could lose herself in the therapeutic act of creating art.

As the days passed, Jennifer's confidence grew as she discovered a newfound sense of self through her artwork. She found purpose and meaning in the swirls and strokes of her paintbrush, crafting a vibrant world that reflected her inner hopes and dreams. The process became a healing ritual, each brushstroke a silent plea for understanding and a means to confront the darkness that had enveloped her.

With each painting, a little piece of Jennifer's soul found its place in the world. The prospect of translating her inner struggles into tangible art empowered her, and a sense of purpose emerged from the chaos. Desiree's unwavering support created a safe space for Jennifer's creativity to thrive, and their bond deepened with each shared experience.

The park, once a mere backdrop to Jennifer's despair, became a witness to her transformation. The vibrant spring air with a gentle breeze provided a soothing atmosphere that complemented her artistic endeavors. As the sun set earlier each day, the warm glow of the studio's windows illuminated the path of her recovery, a tangible sign of hope amidst the encroaching darkness.

Jennifer's artistic outlet and the encouragement from her sister provided a much-needed interruption to her inner demons. The clouds of depression, though still present, seemed to loosen their grip, as if the gentle wind had found its way into the rigid confines of her mind. With each new painting, a sense of accomplishment and satisfaction brought a smile to her face, a welcome change from the frowns of despair that had recently become familiar.

The battle against the shadows of her mind was far from over, but Jennifer's determination, coupled with the soothing solace of art, offered a refreshing glimpse of clarity. As her paintings began to take shape, reflecting her inner struggles and hopes, Jennifer felt a heightened sense of accomplishment. The studio's quietude provided the perfect setting for Jennifer's inner storm.

As time moved forward, Jennifer's artistic repertoire grew, and with it, a subtle shift in her perspective. The once bleak world around her took on new meanings, as if the hues of her paintings had begun to influence her perception. The bustling city, which had once mirrored her soul's gloom, now held hints of promise, a reflection of the hope that art had brought into her life.

Yet, Jennifer knew that her recovery was delicate, and the psychiatrist's guidance remained a crucial element in her journey. The medications and regular sessions provided a framework for her growth, supporting the cerebral neurotransmitter shifts that were taking place. She felt the depressive symptoms alleviating and she gained more energy and vitality.

The city's vibrant nightlife, once a mere blur to Jennifer, now held a certain allure. One evening, as she and Desiree strolled along the river, the city's reflections glistened in the water's surface, and Jennifer felt a strange sense of connection. The beauty of the skyline's silhouette seemed to echo the landscapes emerging on her canvas. It was as if the world had begun to speak to her, revealing secrets that only the discerning eye could detect.

Jennifer's artistic exploration became a beacon, illuminating the path towards her rebirth. As the old Jennifer shed her layers, a new one emerged, shaped by the healing powers of art and the unwavering support of her sister. The battle against mental illness was an ongoing one, but the hope kindled within her soul burned brightly, a promise of a renewed life filled with color and meaning.

As Jennifer continued her artistic exploration, finding solace in the creative sanctuary of Desiree's art studio, an intriguing twist unfolded. A close friend of Desiree, an enigmatic figure named Sebastian, took notice of Jennifer's captivating paintings, particularly a striking portrait capturing the essence of a troubled soul. Intrigued by the depth of emotion conveyed, Sebastian offered to sponsor Jennifer's first solo exhibition, a gesture of support for the arts and a platform to showcase her talents.

The exhibition, titled "Resurrection," reflected Jennifer's journey of healing and self-discovery through art. Each painting told a chapter of her story, the vibrant hues and intricate details offering a glimpse into her inner world. The exhibition created a buzz in the artistic community, attracting critics and enthusiasts alike, all captivated by the raw emotion and resilience depicted in

Jennifer's work.

Among the attendees was an influential art critic, Elaine, known for her discerning eye and powerful reviews. Elaine was deeply moved by Jennifer's exhibition, seeing it as a testament to the transformative power of art. Her favorable review, propelled Jennifer into the limelight.

As the therapeutic endeavors further progressed, the psychiatrist witnessed the resilience of the human spirit—an indomitable force that could overcome even the darkest trials. Jennifer's story, though fraught with pain, became a testament to the enchanting and enduring power of sustained hope and the profound strength ingrained within our minds.

THE BLIND SCIENTIST

An intriguing tale unfolded at the intersection of science and tragedy as John, a brilliant scientist, found his world plunged into darkness following an accidental explosion in his laboratory. The loss of his sight was a devastating blow. As John grapples with this new reality, the weight of his sightless future bears down on him, fueling his anguish.

John's research, was aimed at curing cancer, driven by the ambition to find a cure for cancer, a disease that had claimed his mother's life years ago. He was determined to make a breakthrough that could save lives and honor his family's memory.

The accident stole John's sight, plunging him into a deep well of despair and leaving him grappling with the sudden loss. The added sad news of his father's passing served as a catalyst to sending him into a deeper spiral of depression.

The accident stole John's sight, plunging him into a deep well of despair and leaving him grappling with the sudden loss. The added sad news of his father's passing served as a catalyst to sending him into a deeper spiral of depression.

John, stumbled through his darkened world. The accident was plunging him into a deep abyss of despair, a bottomless pit that threatened to swallow him whole. To make matters worse, the news of his father's passing further catalyzed his descent into a profound depression. John's once vibrant world had faded into darkness, and the weight of his future sightless existence bore down on him with an overwhelming force.

John spent most of his time in bed, the pain of his loss amplified by the silence that enveloped him. John's health was rapidly deteriorating, a stark reminder of the toll this tragic event had taken on his body and mind. The memory of his father's warm embrace and guiding presence was a ghost that haunted him, adding fuel to the flames of his despair.

John's brother, Peter, and a nurse's aide, Aida, tried their best to care for him. They helped him navigate his apartment, but John's despair was all-encompassing. He isolated himself, feeling hopeless and overwhelmed by the darkness that seemed to intensify with each passing day. As his mental state deteriorated, so did his physical well-being, leaving him bedridden and frail.

The explosive incident not only stole John's sight but also thrust him into a profound pit of despair. As John stumbled through his sightless world, his physical and mental health rapidly deteriorated; each day was a struggle against the relentless anguish that consumed him.

As the days grew longer, the pain of John's condition grew more profound, and hope seemed to evaporate with the passing time. John's routine now consisted of slow, painstaking walks around the garden with his brother, Peter, who did his best to raise his spirits. The fragrant flowers provided a fleeting moment of inspiration amidst the gloom.

On days when Peter was occupied with work, John found solace in the company of Aida, a nurse's aide who shared stories of her family's strong history with cancer. The news of her sister's recent demise from the disease served as an additional reminder for John of the fragility of life. John's world had shrunk to the confines of his apartment, his once bustling life now a distant memory. The silence that enveloped him was deafening, amplifying the pain of his losses.

The brief respite from his despair came during the rare

occasions when Peter or Aida read to him, their voices a welcome intrusion into the quiet. They would gather around him, their warm presence a temporary relief from the cold grip of loneliness. Despite the unwavering support of his brother and Aida, John's mental and physical health continued to deteriorate. The weight of his blindness and the tragic loss of his parents bore down on him, an insurmountable burden that sapped his strength with each passing day. The hours spent alone in his cold apartment intensified his feelings of hopelessness, and the thought of a sightless future was almost too much to bear.

The consulting psychiatrist, attuned to the intricacies of the human psyche, recognized the depth of John's depression and the immediate need for intervention. The situation was critical: John's appetite waned, his energy ebbed, and his sleep was fitful and disturbed. With each passing day, the prospect of continuing seemed increasingly bleak.

An intensive treatment plan was devised, centered around a powerful antidepressant to alleviate the relentless grip of the deeply penetrating depression symptoms. The psychiatrist's expertise guided John through the labyrinth of his mind, helping him challenge the dark thoughts that threatened to consume him.

The treatment's effectiveness was gradual, but with each passing week, a subtle shift occurred. John's appetite returned, his energy levels began to stabilize, and the clouds of severe depression lifted slightly, offering a glimpse of hope.

Slowly, John began to look forward to Aida's assistance. Her kind words and reassuring presence offered him a glimpse of warmth in the chilling darkness. With each passing day, a subtle shift occurred, and John's determination to recover ignited. The prospect of improving his health began to seem possible.

The psychiatrist's objective perspective painted a clearer picture of John's situation, seeing beyond the immediate tragedy. They delved into the roots of his anguish, uncovering the driving force behind his research—the loss of his mother to cancer years ago. John's determination to cure the disease and save countless lives had fueled his ambition, only to be derailed by this unforeseen setback.

Understanding the intricate web of John's motivations gave the psychiatrist a new angle of approach. Together, they explored the legacy of his mother's influence and the prospect of honoring her memory through his work. It was a slow journey, but with each session, John's sense of purpose began to resurface. The clouds of despair lifted, and a flicker of determination ignited within him.

As John's health began to improve, his determination grew stronger. The prospect of continuing his research, albeit in a different capacity, became a driving force. Assisted by cutting-edge technology, John's passion for his work rekindled. He found new ways to contribute to the cancer research puzzle, using his expertise and a renewed sense of purpose.

Using modified keyboards and Braille input devices, John's fingers danced across the keys, guided by an incredible memory and an unyielding desire to make a difference. With each keystroke, he challenged the limitations of his blindness, refusing to let darkness define him. As he persevered, John's resolve strengthened, and his spirit remained unwavering.

John sought assistance from fellow scientists, contributing remotely to experiments and discussions. His passion for his work and a renewed sense of purpose kindled a flame of hope within him, offering respite from the relentless despair. John's determination grew with each small success, and his influence on his peers was evident. They were inspired by his unwavering spirit and exceptional memory, providing him with the support and resources required for his journey.

As John tackled the complexities of his new situation, the psychiatrist, an ever-present guide, witnessed his remarkable resilience. Together, they explored the psychological intricacies of this rebirth, helping John navigate the emotions that accompanied his newfound hope. The psychiatrist, awestruck by John's strength, gained a deeper understanding of the human mind's incredible ability to adapt and rise above adversity.

John's determination to fight the darkness of his despair grew stronger with each passing day. The prospect of contributing to the greater good through cancer research was a driving force behind his recovery. Working closely with his dedicated research colleagues, John delved deeper into the mysterious genetic codes that were linked to a rare form of the disease. This particular type of cancer carries an infamous reputation for undermining the body's immune system, aggressively accelerating its progression.

Unraveling these complex genetic mysteries ignited a renewed sense of purpose in John. He felt a strong sense of duty to honor his mother's memory and help save countless lives. John's enthusiasm for his work was infectious, and his colleagues were inspired by his unwavering commitment and remarkable memory. Together, they ventured into uncharted territories, collaborating on innovative experiments aimed at cracking the intricate cancer genetic codes. As John's health continued to improve, his appetite for life returned. The clouds of depression that had once shrouded his vision lifted, and a world of possibility opened up before him. With each small success, his determination grew, and the impact of his work became increasingly clear.

John's contributions, combined with the collective efforts of his team, led to a significant breakthrough. They unlocked the secrets of the enigmatic genetic sequences, uncovering their role in the rare cancer's treatment development. This discovery was a pivotal moment, shedding light on new avenues for treatment and offering a beacon of hope for those affected.

The world of cancer research witnessed a paradigm shift as this collective effort yielded fruits, paving the way for newfound optimism and potential life-saving treatments. John's story, a testament to resilience, served as a guiding light, illuminating the path for others navigating the complex realm of scientific inquiry and personal struggles. John's journey is a shining inspirational example of the enduring power of hope and perseverance.

THE DEDICATED ACCOUNTANT

Sam, a dedicated accountant, found his world suddenly upended. The impending tax season, usually a busy time, was now overshadowed by a personal tragedy. His beloved dog, Charlie, a constant companion, was hit by a car, an accident that left him devastated. The loss of his four-legged friend, a gift from his late father, was a painful blow, and Sam struggled to find solace. The empty silence of his home weighed heavily on Sam's heart. The memories of Charlie's playful spirit and the countless hours they had spent together in the park were now mere reminders of his absence. Sam's grief was profound, a dark cloud that followed him as he went about his daily routine.

Sam's routine was now void of its former joy. The park, once a haven of happiness, now held only painful reminders of Charlie's absence. He couldn't shake the profound sense of loss, a weight that pressed down on him with every step. The silence of his home echoed with the memory of Charlie's playful spirit, a stark reminder of the void left by his beloved dog.

Grief consumed Sam, manifesting as a thick fog that obscured his ability to find solace. He felt a profound sense of despair, his heart heavy with the realization that things would never be the same. The accident's impact went deeper than he could imagine, leaving him emotionally vulnerable and withdrawn. The initial shock gave way to a profound sadness that overshadowed the accountant's world.

The dedicated accountant, Sam, stood tearful before the cremation urn containing Charlie's remains. The somber reality of his loss hit home as he stared at the urn, a tangible symbol of the void left by his beloved companion. The loss of his beloved companion, Charlie, plunged Sam into a deep well of despair. It was as if a dark curtain had been drawn across his joyful world, leaving behind only somber memories. The park, once a haven of warmth and laughter, echoed with the hollow reminders of Charlie's absence.

Sam's grief was a tangible presence, a thick fog that followed him everywhere. He felt a profound sense of denial, as if the accident that took Charlie's life had occurred in some alternate reality. The weight of his loss was overwhelming, a constant companion that reminded him of the void left behind.

Sam found himself reliving the joyful moments shared with his puppy, from his early days of mischievous adventures to their more recent park walks. The realization that those moments would remain only as memories hit him like a ton of bricks.

Anger crept into Sam's heart, a bitter taste that left him searching for someone to blame. He felt cheated by the cruel twist of fate that took Charlie away. His eyes darted between the indifferent passing strangers, searching for a semblance of justice. Yet, the world outside remained oblivious to his pain, leaving him feeling isolated in his anguish.

Bargaining crept into the corners of his mind, whispering delusional promises. What if he could turn back time? What if he could have protected Charlie from the cruel fate that befell him? The what-ifs tortured Sam, keeping him awake at night, wracked with guilt and second guesses.

As the reality of his loss began to sink in, a deep depression settled over Sam like a heavy cloak. The once-lively accountant withdrew into himself, becoming a mere shell of his former self.

The joyful spark in his eyes faded, replaced by a somber gaze that reflected the soul-crushing sadness within. He wandered through the motions of his daily routine, mechanical and detached, unable to find comfort in the familiar. The empty silence of his home echoed Charlie's absent bark, a constant reminder of the gaping hole in his life. Charlie's cinerary urn remained a constant, solemn sentinel of Sam's unwavering grief.

The empty silence of his home, a stark contrast to the lively atmosphere he once knew, amplified his incessant despair. As Sam sank deeper into darkness, the workload piled up, adding a new layer of stress to his already fragile state.

The thought of joining Charlie in the great beyond crossed his mind as the sadness and loneliness intensified. Yet, a glimmer of hope remained, a spark ignited by the prospect of finding solace in the understanding and companionship of his sister, Carol. Though separated by distance, the bond between Sam and Carol remained unbreakable, a beacon of light amidst the encroaching gloom.

Sam's sister, Carol, witnessed her brother's descent into darkness. Unable to work and neglecting his own well-being, Sam's health rapidly deteriorated. Concerned for his welfare, Carol urged him to seek help from a psychiatrist. She knew that the understanding and company she could provide were not enough to break through the thick fog of Sam's grief.

The psychiatrist delved deep into the mind of the despondent accountant, Sam. The roots of his despair ran deep, and the psychiatrist's objective perspective painted a dire picture. Sam's world had crumbled around him, the loss of his loyal companion, Charlie, plunging him into a deep well of grief from which he saw no escape. The void left by Charlie's absence was overwhelming, a constant reminder of the joy that once was.

As the psychiatrist continued the session, they uncovered the profound impact of the accident. For Sam, the shock and sadness had evolved into a deep depression, a familiar monster that had consumed him before. The memory of his dog's passing and the lingering sense of inadequacy intensified his anguish. Sam's mental health deteriorated rapidly, mirroring the decline of his physical well-being. The once vibrant accountant was now a shell of himself, his hopes and dreams dwindling with each passing day.

The psychiatrist recognized the urgency of the situation. Sam's despair was all-encompassing, threatening to consume him entirely. Immediate intervention was required to save him from the abyss. They crafted an intensive treatment plan, a lifeline thrown into the depths of his despair. The antidepressant medication would help alleviate the deeply dark clouds shrouding his mind, but it was Sam's determination and the support of his sister, Carol, that would be the true saviors.

The psychiatrist's objective perspective offered a glimmer of hope amidst Sam's deep depression. There was acknowledgement of the profound impact of Charlie's loss. Together, they worked to navigate the intricate web of emotions, helping Sam challenge the thoughts that imprisoned him. It was a slow journey, but with each session, a subtle shift occurred, igniting a flicker of determination within Sam.

As Sam's health began to improve, his perspective began to change. The once-joyful spark in his eyes returned, and a renewed sense of purpose emerged. The thought of joining Charlie in the great beyond still haunted him, but the prospect of honoring his memory through his work offered solace. Sam found purpose in the notion that he could make a difference, even in the aftermath of tragedy.

The psychiatrist's unwavering guidance and Sam's determination became a dynamic duo, paving a road to recovery. Amidst the sorrow, a subtle shift began to emerge. Sam found himself drawn to the soothing tranquility of the park; the very place that had once been imbued with Charlie's playful spirit. He sought solace in the gentle breeze, flowering trees, and the soothing sounds of nature, finding a momentary reprieve from the pain that enveloped him.

The park bench, a witness to many joyful moments, became Sam's sanctuary. He sat motionless, lost in his thoughts, as the sun slowly set, casting a golden hue over the landscape. The beauty of nature, so recently appreciated by Charlie, now offered a fragile bridge between Sam's present and past. Each visit to this cherished spot became a quiet ritual, a tentative step towards acceptance and a gradual reconciliation with his new reality.

The end of each day brought a sense of peace, as if Charlie's spirit found solace in the serene atmosphere of the park's twilight hours. Sam's grief remained, but the edges softened, and a flicker of hope ignited within him. The park, a living testament to the enduring power of memory, offered a quiet invitation to heal and find a new normal amidst the shadows of the past.

Sam's sessions delved into the intricate web of emotions, helping him confront the thoughts that bound him to the past. With each difficult conversation, he grew more determined to channel his energy into aiding those grappling with similar struggles. The psychiatrist's guidance and Sam's unwavering resolve paved the way for a remarkable transformation. Outside the confines of the therapy room, Sam embarked on a new journey. He threw himself into community work, becoming an active listener and a source of support for those grappling with the misfortunes of grief and loss. Sam's experiences had gifted him with a unique perspective, enabling him to offer insight and guidance to those in need. He would take part of a grief support group. His story, one of profound grief and healing, served as a testament to the power of hope and the potential for a renewed sense of purpose.

The park, once a place of joy, became a sanctuary for Sam's

healing. Here, amidst the tranquil surroundings, he found a sense of peace and a slow acceptance of his loss. The memory of Charlie lived on, a constant reminder of the strength and courage required to move forward. As Sam's health improved, his determination to make a difference grew stronger.

The prospect of honoring Charlie's memory through acts of kindness kindled a new fire within him. Each day brought new challenges but also new opportunities to turn adversity into something meaningful. Sam's journey, while unique, reflected the common human capacity for resilience in the face of tragedy.

The accountant's story, a narrative of deep sorrow and rebirth, echoed in the lives of many. Through his experiences, Sam inadvertently became a beacon of hope, illuminating the path for others navigating the complex terrain of grief and personal trials. And so, his tale continued, an enduring testament to the indomitable human spirit.

EPILOGUE

The enigmatic world of depression unfolded before the curious eyes of researchers and clinicians, a complex web of circumstances and brain alterations. It was a mysterious disorder that enveloped its victims, leaving them shrouded in darkness. Amidst this gloom, the resilient human spirit shines through, with some courageously battling the shadows in their minds and others emerging as survivors. The journey towards understanding depression is a treacherous one, an emotional rollercoaster filled with hope and despair.

The cloud of depression lingers over the heads of the afflicted, an enigmatic disorder with its causes being a complex web, a mysterious tangle of circumstances, genetic predispositions, and changes in the brain. These factors are merely the visible tips of an intricate iceberg, beneath which lay a labyrinth of potential triggers.

The accounts of David, Mark, Tina, Anne, Bob, Jennifer, John, and Sam are a demonstration to the complex nature of clinical depression. Each character found themselves entangled in the intricate web of this crippling mental condition, battling the relentless onslaught of symptoms. Their stories, though unique, echo a common narrative of profound struggle and the enduring power of human hope and resilience. The weight of their pasts and present circumstances bore down on them, fueling their anguish.

Yet, amidst the darkness, glimmers of hope emerged, often in the form of supportive companions and the expertise of mental health professionals. The tales of these individuals highlighted the multifaceted nature of depression's causes and its profound impact on their lives. For some, the demons stemmed from traumatic events, while others grappled with the intricate interplay of genetic predispositions and life circumstances. The psychiatrists' trained eyes delved deep into the labyrinth of their minds, unearthing the roots of their despair and offering a beacon of hope amidst the storm. As new research progressed, the understanding of this enigmatic disorder evolved, paving the way for better treatments and an increased chance at recovery. These stories became a testament to the human spirit's indomitable nature and the power of determination in the face of adversity.

Researchers and clinicians alike braved this complex puzzle, driven by a determination to help those engulfed by the disorder. They continue to engage in a relentless pursuit to understand the unique experiences of those suffering from clinical depression. Some of the people affected are warriors, engaging in a relentless struggle against the darkness within their minds. Others emerged as survivors, their resilience a testament to the human spirit.

The tales of individuals grappling with the depths of depression weaved an intricate tapestry, their personal struggles intertwined through striking similarities. Their struggles are uniquely personal yet interconnected through common themes of loss, obsession, and the quest for purpose.

David, a young man plagued by anxiety and restlessness, found himself confined to a COVID-19 isolation ward during the pandemic. His struggles were deep-seated, rooted in the loss of his older brother, which had plunged him into a profound grief that the pandemic had amplified. The darkness that consumed him reflected the intricate web of clinical depression, a complex puzzle that nurse Sarah strived to unravel. As David's condition deteriorated, Sarah's requested a psychiatric consultation which changed David's severe depression and helped him regain hope and ultimately remission. David's story, a tragic narrative of despair, revealed the enigmatic nature of clinical depression, painting a vivid picture of the disorder's far-reaching consequences.

Mark, the haunted executive, found peace in the company of like-minded individuals within a self-help group. Their shared experiences mirrored each other's, a testament to the power of collective healing.

Tina's close encounter with death due to her social media obsession served as a stark reminder of the delicate balance between virtual and real-life connections. Her world had nearly crumbled under the weight of her online existence, the lines between both realms blurring dangerously. But the timely intervention of her concerned friend, Jane, offered a glimpse of hope amidst the darkness.

Anne's own struggles after her traumatic accident found solace in the soothing tranquility of nature. The garden she tended with her sister, Amanda, became a sanctuary, a peaceful oasis amidst the chaos of her recovery. It was a place where the weight of her pain momentarily lifted, and a sense of purpose emerged from the beauty of blooming flowers.

Bob, faced with the uncertainty of unemployment, discovered a new passion in the pizza parlor. The prospect of learning new culinary skills ignited a fire within him, and the thought of contributing to society through his cuisine brought a renewed sense of hope.

Jennifer, battling the inner demons of depression, found an unexpected sanctuary in art. The creative solace offered by Desiree's art studio became a beacon of light, guiding Jennifer towards a path of self-discovery and acceptance. Her exhibition, a bold statement of resilience, resonated with viewers, propelling her into the world of artistic recognition.

The blind scientist, John, persevered in his quest to cure cancer, undeterred by the dual blows of blindness and his father's passing. His determination to make a difference ignited a flame of hope, a driving force that propelled him through the complexities of his new situation. Assisted by cutting-edge technology and the support of fellow researchers, John's passion remained unwavering.

Lastly, Sam, the devastated accountant, found purpose in the aftermath of his beloved dog's tragic death. The void left by Charlie's absence was immeasurable, but Sam channeled his energy into supporting others who shared his pain. The park, once a place of joy, became a symbolic setting for his healing, where the memory of Charlie lived on.

These recounts, unique in their specifics yet interconnected through common themes, showcased the resilience of the human spirit. Amidst the chaos and darkness, the enduring power of hope prevailed. It was a testament to the enduring strength within us, a silent reminder that even in the face of adversity, the sun would eventually break through the clouds.